Humans at Work

By

*in alphabetical order, because science
is a co·operative effort in which there is no room for petty considerations
of personal glory, and, anyway, we're not so sure that
everyone pulled his weight here.*

**Mike Dowdall
Dennis Welch
Pat Welch**

Watercolor by
Melinda May Sullivan

*with help from the
above-named, which slowed
her down considerably.*

A FIRESIDE BOOK
Published by Simon & Schuster, Inc.
New York

Ack

and oremost, we want to thank
our paste-up artists, who have done
such a f   job on *Hum   at Work,* as
well as our previous book,

Their work is behind the scenes and
not often recognized, but it is extr
impo tant. If it is not done conscientio
and correctly, the little p c s of type
will ft   fail to adhere to the page,
resulting in emb   assing omissions or
alterations. So here's to you,   ni r
    dgl ,   ecky ib , and   s
Thanks, and, as usual, your checks
are   ma l.

    turally, there are a great many other
p ople without   and
book   not have been possible, since
we would pr
and get real jobs a long time ago.

            , of course, is our
ed tor,   rb   ffn , whose judge-
ment   nd guidance were so c nsistent-
ly valuable to us that   why
people   started s ying those things
about him.   seemed so small and
un   ry. Ot ers who must be
s ngled out inclu   eck   ,   ick
    nie, Al   arl   all,
Sr.,   ow   Jr., a y oo y,
P   y   r, rv   oy   rr
  ri   la , J   s   g   h,
      a   v e, J   at   e n e
O   ,   s   , oe n
    lc   e   oa   e, om
a   ag   ess   , an
  en   , V   ill ,
M r   is   ot   el

        ,   ,   ,
    rg   ek   ,   cl ,   ga
      ,   ey   ow , ei
      , he   er   il ,   ry   d
Do   t,   ymo   t, mm
  y   ,   ul el   , eff   n   ,
    n   ol   ,   lta   q   ,
g   fr   ng i, and,   but by
no means least, our pa nts.

The usual difficulty with acknowledge-
ments, of course, is that someone is
inevitably   t. We have tak n great
care to avoid that unfortunate

For once, we are confident that no one
has been p ssed over.

Contents

Introduction

Since the publication of our extensive field research among the humans (*Humans,* Simon & Schuster, 1984), the reading public at large as well as the scientific community has, understandably, clamored for more information about these extraordinary beings. Our difficulty in responding to this demand was not that we lacked additional information; on the contrary, we could have filled several books of weighty aspect and still hardly have scratched the surface of all that is marvelous and strange about the lives of the humans. Our problem was one of narrowing the subject down.

As we had done so many times in the past when faced with such a quandary, or whenever we felt like spending a few days in one of the nicer hotels near the park, we turned to our publishers for advice and guidance. We were not disappointed. From our discussions with them came, in addition to the intimation that there might be such a thing as abusing room service, the idea that what was wanted was not merely more, but more *specific* information about human life and customs. In fact, they said, warming to the possibilities, an entire book dealing with one of the more colorful areas of human behavior may be just the ticket.

They dispensed a great many other useful tips and suggestions, and in all cases we listened attentively. (It is an old human belief that failing to act on suggestions from your publisher will cause something to go wrong in the accounting department, or with the mail. Superstition? Perhaps. But when you have lived among the humans for as long as we have, you can't help but pick these things up.)

We checked out discreetly, signed the bill, and returned to our notes, much uplifted by our new-found sense of direction, and eager to begin planning our next collection of observations. Clearly, we reasoned, the area we chose for detailed examination must be one that was common to all, or nearly all, humans. Equally clearly, it must be an aspect of behavior which could be considered central to their lives. And obviously it must be one which translated well in terms of coloring book adaptations, plush toys, and coffee mugs, to say nothing of poster and video rights. With these criteria in mind, we began to extend ourselves along the lines of possible themes.

Humans, we had already observed, are an unusually mobile group, suggesting the feasibility of such a treatise as *Aspects of Some Human Modes of Transportation.* Though the academic dignity of the title was undeniable, brief reflection told us that this was a subject which had pretty much been done. *The Big Book of Wheels* came to mind, for instance, or *Airport.*

However, we had also spent quite some time researching human eating habits, and we knew that food was a concern which could be said to be common to most humans. Perhaps we should be leaning in the direction of a cookbook, or definitive restaurant guide. This idea was supported by a recent letter in the op-ed page complaining of the difficulty in finding a good human restaurant, while every other street corner seemed to offer the usual Mandarin or Szechuan. Eventually, however, we rejected this plan on the grounds that (a) we may have misunderstood the letter, and (b) as serious research scientists, we could hardly expect to be considered credible as chefs. A disappointment, since we had felt that our tentative title, *Humans At Wok*, had a nice ring to it.

Another likely subject, and one which had the advantage that anyone can write books about it without troubling over credentials, was sex. This seemed to have possibilities, and another look at our notes indicated that here was an area in which the humans were anything but reticent: raw material would be no problem. But a brief perusal of the fall catalogues told us that the bookstores were already up to their remainders in sex books. We had no wish to appear unoriginal.

In short, we soon found ourselves in a slightly different version of our original dilemma, and saw nothing for it but to place another appeal for guidance with our publishers.

"How," we queried, "considering the rich and complex tapestry of genuinely incomprehensible behavior which makes up the human character, would you suggest we actually go about choosing a specific theme?"

"In essence," they said, "we feel that it is your job to write books and ours to publish them. What we would suggest is that you do your job, and we will do ours."

And there, of course, it was.

A response to certain so-called "critics."

Humans at Work, like its predecessor, *Humans,* is a serious scientific inquiry, produced with sober objectives in mind: to enrich the stores of anthropological knowledge; to extend the frontiers of science; and to justify a deduction of $9,127.56 for typewriter ribbons, which has become the source of some small controversy. This is, no doubt, a misunderstanding which we are sure can be cleared up through reasonable discussion. But we digress.

The point is that, despite our repeated statements of solemn and scholarly purpose, we have been criticized in certain quarters for what has been called "frivolousness," "commercialism," and even "exploitation." One critic went so far as to use the phrase "frivolous commercial exploitation," thereby more or less summing up the views of his colleagues.

We can only conclude that there exists a group of pompous, pseudo-intellectual snobs who would perpetuate the idea that if a scientific publication happens to result in a line of coffee mugs, a few plush toys, an HBO special or two, and one lousy licensing deal for a line of fashion activewear, then said publication cannot be considered "serious."

Ordinarily, we wouldn't lower ourselves to respond to such spurious nitpicking. It happens, however, that *Humans at Work* contains several features which are so obviously designed to appeal to the more academic turn of mind that we are confident we can lay to rest, once and for all, any trace of doubt as to the scientific and scholarly nature of these works.

The first and most exhaustive of these features is the inclusion of the complete *Encyclopedia of Human Work.* This scholarly catalogue, unabridged and unexpurgated, lists every single kind of work in which humans are known to engage. Each is accompanied by a brief definition and description, and many are illustrated in full color. This seminal work belongs in every home, and is an invaluable field guide for the student and professional anthropologist alike.

The second feature, the *Humans at Work Review Quiz,* will be found distributed throughout the book, with answers and scoring curve on page 106. You may answer each quiz question as you come to it, while the information contained in the applicable section is fresh in your mind, or you may return to the quiz when you have completed the text and take the review as a whole. Or you can just look at the answers, since, after all, there is no one to stop you. We couldn't care less, since getting a perfect score wins you nothing whatever, and completed quizzes which are mailed to us will be thrown away unceremoniously.

The third special feature of *Humans at Work* is one which we feel goes a long way toward including you, the reader, in the excitement and spontaneity of the scientific process.

Naturally, most information gathered in the field is subjected to intense scrutiny. All raw data is researched, verified, cross-checked, or sometimes we just sort of kick it around until it seems like it's probably true, before it is considered for inclusion in the book. There are times, however, when that elusive, electric moment of discovery – the true essence, we feel, of anthropology – seems to get lost in all that processing. You may well imagine, then, our delight when a communique from our publisher disclosed the fact that our final manuscript seemed to be some few pages short of our actual contractual obligation, especially once they decided against our original suggestion of setting the text in 36 point type (an attempt on our part to show some consideration for the golden-agers among our readership, and having nothing to do, as has been snidely suggested, with "padding.")

We immediately decided to make use of this windfall space by including many, if not all, of our original field notes for *Humans at Work*—spontaneous sketches and observations made on the spot, as they happened, and unsullied by all that tedious verification. The flavor, you might say, has been left in. We like to call these features *"Science in Action."*

In the rest of *Humans at Work,* of course, you will find the same meticulous, in-depth observation and analysis that made *Humans* practically a household word.

Not serious? Ha.

SCIENCE IN ACTION Quiz Page

You may be wondering why we are giving you a review quiz before you have had a chance to read anything. This demonstrates a lack of appreciation on your part for the difficulties involved in getting the pages of a book to come out even. Still, we want to be fair, so this first Science in Action Review Quiz will be confined to general knowledge and aptitude. You need not have read this *or any other* book, so this could be your chance to bring your grade up.

A man and his wife.

A man and his wife have spent their life's savings to purchase a horse. They plan to start a circus with the horse as their main attraction. Upon delivery, they discover that their horse has only three legs. Have they any legal recourse?

The old mansion.

A family has moved into the old mansion at the edge of town. The first night, the father hangs himself in the rumpus room. The second night, the children are carried away by a foul-smelling slime-creature. The third night, the dog eats some glass. On the fourth night, the mother hears a noise in the attic. Will she

A. finally get the bejesus out of there;
B. march straight up and investigate, continuing to poke around even after her flashlight is snatched away by an unseen presence, or
C. continue to read her self-help book on dealing with the death of a beloved pet?

Two scalded dogs.

A train is traveling east at 60 mph. It has 36 cars containing 280 passengers who have paid an average fare of $172.00 each, and one hiding in the restroom who has paid nothing. The train is carrying 1,057 pieces of mail, 495 pieces of luggage, two scalded dogs, and a coffin. A truck is traveling west at 45 mph. It is transporting 546 chickens. The driver is 68 years old. His passenger is 22 years old. They hate each other. Which will reach the railroad crossing first?

Surprising facts.

If every man, woman, and child on the planet were laid end to end, what would be the point?

A potato crop.

Old Farmer Gunderson has loaded his only vehicle, a horse-drawn wagon, with his entire potato crop. The only road to the city is a modern superhighway on which horse-drawn wagons are prohibited. How can Old Farmer Gunderson get his potatoes to market?

Farmer Brown.

Farmer Brown owns a cow. Farmer Green owns a barn. Farmer White owns a horse. Farmer Magenta owns a tractor. If Farmer Burnt Sienna owns a pig, and Farmer Cerulean Blue some chickens, what must Farmer Vermilion have in order for them to start a farm?

Optical illusions.

Which policeman is closer, A or B?

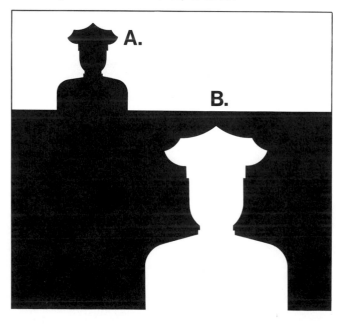

Section One

What is Work; What isn't

What work is; what it isn't.

In the interests of avoiding subsequent confusion, we reasoned that it would probably be a good idea to establish at the outset just what work actually looks like. There would be little point, after all, in our analyzing phenomena which might later turn out to be merely body surfing or competitive spelling–human activities which might *seem* like work to the uninitiated, but which in fact have no place in this study.

We soon discovered the fact that the question is so obscured by shadings and nuances that it might well justify its own separate and complete study. Tedious as that sounds, it is to be remembered that just such exhaustive groundwork is essential to the true scientific method. Still, it sounds *so* tedious that we are sure the reader will understand why we wasted little time in deciding the hell with it.

We have, of course, included such notes and observations as we had completed before electing to get on with the rest of the book. The following is a brief glossary of a few common variations.

On a break

This means that the human in question *was* working recently, and *will be* working soon, but *is not* working at the time that you bring the teddy bear slippers up to the register.

Not my job

This means that the human is considered to be working, but is sick and tired of some people sending teddy bear slippers to Neckwear and Men's Furnishings and you will have to take them to Children's Sleepwear.

Not my department

This is a condition of working selectively, and means that, in the human's judgment, teddy bear slippers cannot be considered sleepwear and must be paid for in Junior Footwear on the third floor.

At lunch

This refers to everyone on the third floor.

Market Analysis

This is a specialized form of work in which a highly trained human analyzes masses of economic and demographic data in order to determine why teddy bear slippers aren't moving.

Relative Levels of Discomfort

Human A wakes to the sound of Human B shrieking on the radio. Between gongs and buzzers, Human B informs Human A that it is 6:27 AM, a time at which no known creature will voluntarily enter a room filled with cold, hard objects, and/or subject itself to complete immersion in water. This, nevertheless, is exactly what Human A does, often taking the radio with him so that Human B is able to continue screaming at him during the process.

(Human B, whose voice emanates from the radio, is actually sitting in a small, well-heated room in a comfortable chair, intermittently flipping switches and honking a bicycle horn.)

Human A, dripping and shivering, continues his mortification of the flesh while listening to Human B report that traffic conditions everywhere range from unreasonable *(buzz, ding)* to intolerable *(honk, whoop-whoop-whoop)*. Human A seems to understand this communication perfectly, and yet he resolves to *leave his home for the express purpose of becoming a part of this situation.*

After 47 minutes of participating in traffic conditions, Human A arrives at the building which contains his office and enters the parking garage, where he will pay $4.50 for every twelve minutes or fraction thereof during which his car is there. He approaches a machine which dispenses a ticket, which is also his contract. By accepting it, he agrees that if he returns and his car is gone, or if it is there but happens to be in flames, it will be okay with him and will not reflect in any way on the people in the garage, whom he will pay the maximum rate.

Through all of this, which human do you suppose is considered to be working? Human B. You *(honk!)* go figure.

Guidelines for the field researcher.

The truth is that our attempts to establish a hard and fast rule for the identification of work vs. non-work came to nothing in the end. It seems there are few, if any, endeavors which are so strenuous, pointless, or humiliating that some human somewhere will not undertake them just for fun.

Still, we were able to formulate certain rough guidelines which, while not infallible, should prove to be useful aids to the field observer.

Fig. 1. The Wearing of Outlandish Uniforms With No Obvious Military Affiliation.

Fig. 2. The Unusual Expenditure of Energy While Nearly Naked.

Fig. 3. The Fitting of Uncomfortable Equipment, Especially to the Head.

If the researcher in the field keeps an eye out for one or more of these conditions, he can be reasonably confident that he is observing a human at work approximately 66% of the time. In science, as in life, two out of three is better than a fire in the glove compartment.

Fig. 1

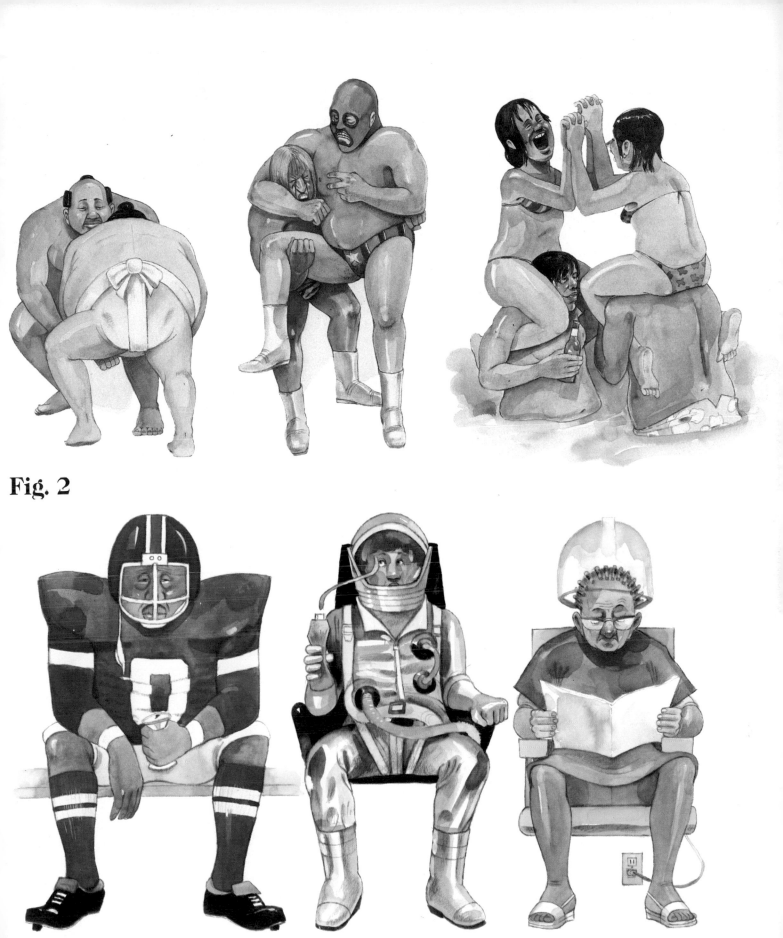

Fig. 2

Fig. 3

Why they do it.

In the course of a life dedicated to scientific research, the professional anthropologist sees a great deal of colorful, even bizarre, behavior. If that same anthropologist has chosen the world of the humans for his particular field of study – well, suffice it to say that words such as "bizarre," "incomprehensible," or "pointless" soon lose their impact. Of course, words like "pointless" don't really have a lot of impact in the first place, but what we mean is, like, remember when you were a little kid and you'd lie in bed and repeat some word over and over? Some simple word like "cake." You'd just lie there in the dark, with your eyes closed, and say – not out loud, just in your head – "Cake, cake, cake, cake, cake, cake, cake," until, when you've said it about a million times, it doesn't mean anything any more? And pretty soon you're not even sure there *is* such a word? Or there is, but it doesn't mean what you think? But

you keep going, "Cake, cake, cake, cake, cake, cake, cake, cake, cake," even though you're really disoriented now. Like if you opened your eyes you wouldn't be in your room. Or you would be, but outside would be some weird landscape, or your whole house would be flying. But you don't open your eyes. By now you don't *dare.* You keep going, "Cake, cake, cake, cake, cake, cake, cake." Then you start to think that your parents might be vampires. You don't know what they do in their room at night, but you have seen some pretty strange artifacts in there during the day. They *could* be vampires. They could be *anything.*

Suddenly you realize you've gone too far, you've been doing this since before the pyramids, your parents *are* vampires and probably planned all your life for you to do exactly what you're doing now, and if you open your eyes you'll probably fall straight *up* or something. You understand nothing, the universe is not at all like you thought. Your whole life has been a horrible joke played on you by forces beyond your comprehension. In the end, though, you just wake up and go to school, and you don't even remember how you got out of it.

In a way, that's kind of what work is like to humans.

Still, we have to admit it doesn't explain why they do it.

18

Quiz Page

Study the human pictured below. From what you have learned in the previous chapter, would you say he is

A. missing the sign from the third base coach that he has been cut from the roster and should not be on deck;

B. wondering why they call it "on deck;"

C. engaging in the great American pastime.

20

Section Two

Rites
of Passage:

From
Childhood to
Work

The true importance of play.

It is, of course, well known to the student of nature that much of what appears to be innocent play among young animals is actually training for the rigors and responsibilities of adulthood. The young tiger cub, for instance, kittenishly stalking its siblings through the grass, is in fact honing the instinctive hunting techniques so necessary to his survival as an adult. Other examples abound, such as the young lion cub kittenishly stalking... well, that's pretty much the same as the tiger cub example. But consider the young, let's say, bear cub–no, that's the same thing, too, isn't it? Still, how many of us, finding that we have foolishly moved into a neighborhood without cable, have watched countless hours of PBS nature shows, including the always popular footage of the young wolf cub playfully leaping on its brothers and sisters from the underbrush? Other, examples, even more widely varied, are too numerous to mention.

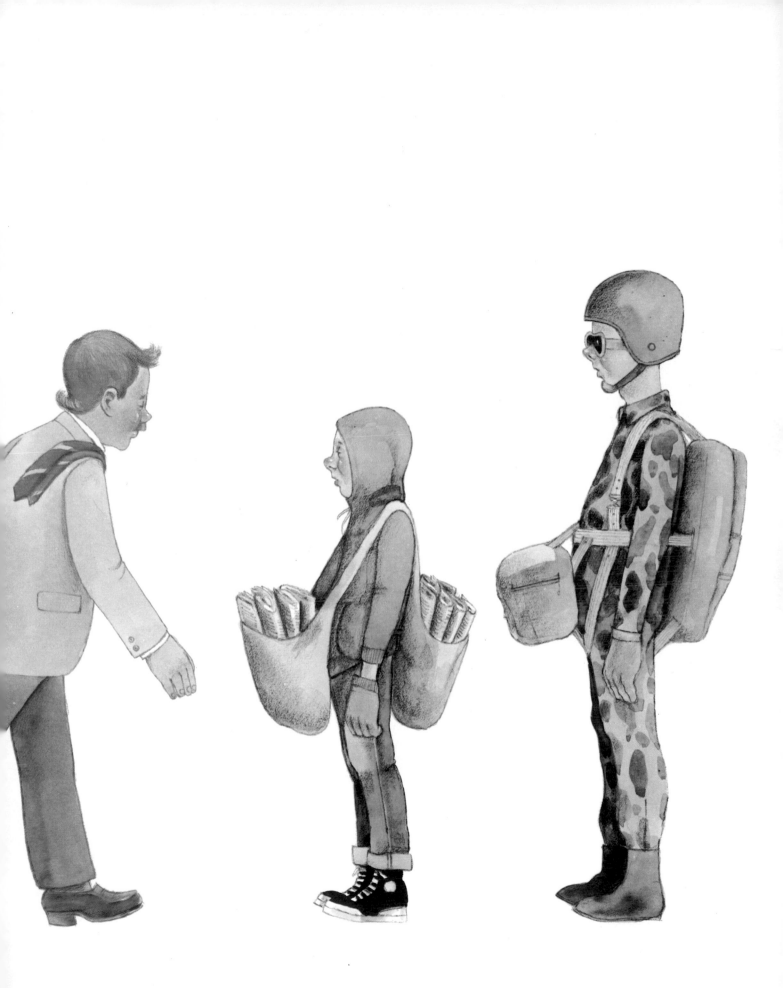

Becoming an Adult Worker – Prayer and Sacrifice

Ritual behavior connected to advancement into adulthood, including prayers, sacrifices, and various mortifications of the flesh, is common to most societies and cultures. Nowhere, however, will you find such streamlined and convenient versions of this behavior as among the humans.

For instance, prayers beseeching the unseen forces for special consideration – an act no doubt familiar to most of us – were once whiningly intoned at the altar of some monstrous idol, probably a form of the toad god. (Primitive societies always have a toad god, possibly because the large mouth is easy to hit with sacrifices, and the tongue makes a good place for the steps.) Far from being intimidated by their bestial deity, however, the humans have, over the millennia, simply scaled him down to manageable size (Fig. 1-3). Now they are found docilely squatting on every corner – we refer, of course, to the toad gods – and favorable hours for sacrifice are clearly posted on each one.

In addition, the traditional prayer itself has been reduced to a simple and more or less universal form (Fig. 4). True, it is still obsequious and insincere, but it would hardly be recognizable as a prayer if it were otherwise. With minor variations, they all ask for the same thing, and in approximately the same language: "Seek challenging position in growth-oriented firm." In human, this may be roughly translated as "clean, undemanding work which elevates prestige without requiring concentration or talent." (The bald-faced aspect of this prayer, some scholars believe, is the reason for the gradual elimination of the eyes from the modern effigies of the toad god.)

Many copies of the prayer – the more, of course, the better – are placed in the toad god-like receptacle, and each is accompanied by a sacrifice of money. Here again, we see the indomitable human will to make things as easy on themselves as possible. The original form of this sacrifice, without doubt, was an offering of some object held to be of value to the primitive human – a clam or favorite root thrown into the fire, or lobbed toward the gaping mouth of the idol. Like the idol and the prayer itself, however, the sacri-

fice has also been refined into a convenient symbol, which can be purchased in sheets or rolls and *affixed directly* to the written supplication. No more confusion as to which sacrifice is intended to support which prayer, something that must have been a major problem for the early toad god.

Convenient and sophisticated as it is, you may be asking yourself, does all this really go any farther than the old primitive methods toward getting the human the desirable work he wants? Actually, there is no evidence that it does. And yet, the humans *believe* that it does, and surely they derive a certain comfort from the ritual itself. What more does any of us need, after all, if we are at peace with our toad god?

Fig. 1

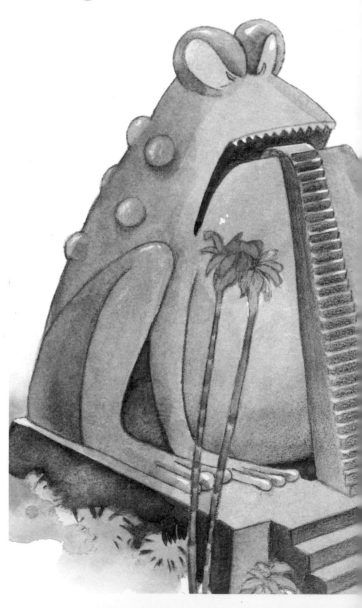

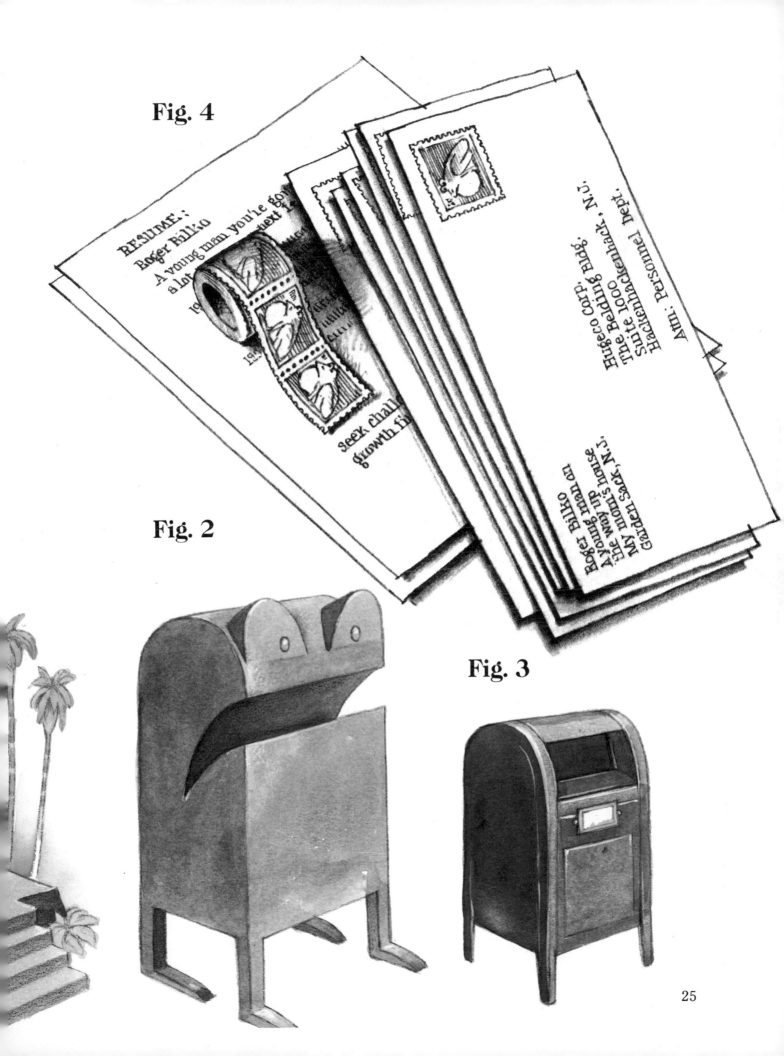

Fig. 4

RESUME:
Roger Bilko
A young man you're go[...]
a lo[...] [...]ext [...]

Seek chall[...]
growth fi[...]

Fig. 2

Hugeco Corp. Bldg., N.J.
The Belding
Suite 1000
Hackenhacken bldg.
Attn: Personnel dept.

Roger Bilko
A young man on
A way up house
My mom's Sack, N.J.
Garden Sack, N.J.

Fig. 3

Odd Jobs in the Arts

Find among the humans a novelist who refuses to produce the hackneyed commercialism demanded by philistine acquiring editors; find an actor whose commitment to relevant drama transcends the narrow imaginations of toadying "popular" directors; seek out the inventor/entrepreneur whose independent vision is undampened by the unwillingness of complacent robber barons to fund his most daring concepts. Do this, and what will you have found? What *we* found was a cab driver, a waiter, and a carwash attendant.

What, we wondered, was the common denominator that must exist between these disparate jobs in the arts? Through an exhaustive series of personal interviews which took us not only into the hearts and minds of these human artists, but also into some pretty strange neighborhoods, we found the surprising answer. Frankly, we expected it to have something to do with independence or artistic integrity. But what it boils down to is that, since very few artists, actors, inventors, or poets can actually afford to keep an apartment, they all naturally gravitate toward jobs which include the use of a locker.

How obvious is the truth, once revealed.

Driver/novelist.

His four-volume avant-garde novel, written from the first-person point of view of the central character's tietack, has already exposed the true venality of even the so-called "literary" publishers, who have actually suggested that he do something "to make it shorter, or somehow less boring." Undaunted, he says, "They laughed at the naturalists, too, until finally they all just went away, or got jobs, or whatever they did."

Painter/messenger.

"The neo-expressionists have been concerned with space, form, and color, and the dynamics of these relationships. My work goes beyond that, dealing with the effects of petroleum-based collodial suspensions more or less smeared over two-dimensional cardboard planes, not really for any particular reason except that you can buy this stuff at any art supply store. That's, you know, my statement."

Derivative? Or the next genuine new vision? Only time will tell, and to a person whose day job brings him into contact with so many opportunities for chemical experimentation, time means very little.

Fashion designer.

"Line! Line is everything. Without line you have only color, form, texture–and zippers! Oh! Oh! Zippers! These things are *clothes.* They are not *fashion.* Fashion is line! Line! Line! Sometimes I shriek in this way at my models, who love it, in a way. To love line is to love *life,* to love *light,* to love, as I do, going out and being *seen!*"

Interpretive dancer.

"For centuries, dance has been seen in only three ways: *moving, gracefully,* and to *music.* My thesis at St. Macramé Mobile College of Arts and Crafts–and all my work since–is dedicated to re-examining these outmoded and irrelevant attitudes. Why should there be sound and motion *on stage,* and silence and stillness in the audience? My first major interpretive ballet, *Flaming Urban Insects,* completely exploded this empty convention when the entire company sat on stage coughing and fidgeting and staring at the audience, who were surprised to find that we had removed the seats and provided 600 radios, each tuned to a different station. Those were four hours that I like to think redefined ballet."

Poet.

"I don't like to talk about my work. I don't like to talk about *anything*. I hate words. Words are the single greatest obstacle to communication. I don't suppose you know what the hell I'm talking about, and why should you? I hate words. I hate people, too. In my recent work, I have completely abandoned words in favor of pure abrasiveness. As you may guess, you can't do really pure wordless abrasiveness in the traditional ways, in books or magazines. You can't set it in type and distribute it to major population centers, riding the bales of pulp like a grinning flea-skull on the scabrous ankle of wino humanity hummingshiningscreaming down the terrifying superhighway America. Sorry. I slipped back into my word period for a second there. Excuse me."

As we have seen, the artists enter their chosen fields, apart from the lockers, because something deep inside prevents them from doing otherwise. There is one other small group who inherit their respective jobs and are not troubled by the need to make any conscious choice (Fig. 1–2). But the great majority of humans must decide for themselves, choosing a specialized area of work based on many considerations, including their own aptitudes, the opportunities for advancement within the field, the probability of meeting broads, and, of course, the question of whether they will be required to buy special shoes.

Virtually all humans who lack an uncle in the union make this decision through the medium of the public document reproduced on the following pages – but they do not do this hastily. As you might expect, the reading of these employment opportunity listings is an act so surrounded by ceremony that it may well be the most rigidly stylized of all areas of human work behavior.

For example, not only will the job-seeking human not read the listings without another human present (this may be his mother or his sister's husband, depending on where he has been living since junior college), he will not even unfold the paper unless the Three Stooges are on, he has a beer at his elbow, and no more than 25 minutes have elapsed since he last ate.

With so much ritual to be observed, it sometimes seems surprising that so many promising careers are launched at all.

Fig. 1-2

ESCORTS

CONTINENTAL escort service. Cultured, refined, discreet companions who will pretend they don't mind your breath. Call 415-WHOO.

J.C.'S ESCORTS. In town for a diplomatic dinner and just discovered you brought your white tie and medals but left your charming and gracious wife at home? Yeah, I know how it is, Chief. I used to be a courtier to the Sun King myself. Cut the crap and pick up the phone. 212-BRDS.

MADAME BIMBEAU. Highly educated and refined young ladies, many models, actresses, contortionists. Wherever you wish to go, they've been. Guaranteed to be taller than you are. 607-BMBO.

MASSAGE

AFRICAN Massage. Different. Restless. Rhythmic. Ask for Toby.

ALL-OUT massage. You only need one.

AMERICAN massage. You know what an American massage is, don't you? Well, I guess I can't tell you here, but the punch line is, "Well, in that case, how about a quarter pounder?" Get it?

ASIAN massage. Inscrutable; perilous.

MEN'S massage. For men. By men. With men. No towels. Ask for David.

ORIENTAL massage. Ask for Bubba.

ORGANIC massage. Celery juice and real manure. Prolongs life, privacy.

OUTCALL massage. Bambi.

OUTCALL massage. Brandi.

OUTCALL massage. Candi.

Fess. I am going to roll myself up in a great big ball and fly. That's life. Guy.

Anyone witnessing serious, fatal accident 4/16 at corner 12th and Figaroa. pls. contact Dan W. P.O. Box 7, this paper. I wasn't involved, I just want to have a couple of beers and talk about it. Did you see the blood? I could have sworn I saw a hand fly through the air. I almost barfed. Sheesh!

Anyone who knows the whereabouts of my car pls. contact Phil at the Gristle Pit 7th and B St. Sure, it's happened before, but this time it isn't funny. It's been three days. I can't even find anybody who saw me that night. I swear, this is the last time.

B. Come home. I wasn't finished with you and you know it. R.

BUSINESS OPPORTUNITIES

FACING bankruptcy? Can't make payments? Out of work? Boy, that's rough, kid. Let me know if things work out. Concerned, P.O. Box 19, Falling Rock, Wyoming.

HYPNOTIZE your way to health, fortune, borderline social acceptability. My book tells how to make total strangers hand over purses, wallets, underthings. Send $14.95 to: I'm Sleepy, You're Dopey, P.O. Box 5, Mandrake, LA.

RICHES: In three short weeks I can make you a millionaire. How? Send me $1.00 and in three short weeks receive my book. It worked for me, why not for you? Do you think I'm any smarter than you are? So do I. Prove it by sending $1.00 to: Buck Fulminster, P.O. Box 16, Humidor, AZ.

STUCK in a low-paying job? Consider the Lesser Antilles!

---

room, etc. Excellent fringe benefits as they often forget to lock their rooms. Apply in person to: Geezers and Things, 628 St. Coot Place, Altzheimer, CA.

BOOKBINDER Must be half-mad, near-blind. Pref. usual wispy white hairs hanging listlessly over frayed collar; pathetic, obscure lifetime of exp. Grub & Dickens Publishers, Aardvark-on-the-Sharkbite, Kidney Walls, G.B.

ACTUARY Min 5 yrs. exp. with major insurance carrier. Degree pref. Record of accuracy a must. Short-term employment. Actually, we just want to know when we're going to die. Box 21, c/o this paper.

ADMIN ASST. Fin. dist. co. common min. A/RA/P exp. w/mo type AR/F min. wpm 1 yr. Hlp. us fig. our wht. we mean. Res. only to: MD/SIC/Post Min/Inc. c/o this paper.

ADVERTISING SALES New magazine for fastest-growing special-interest group in U.S. needs proven self-starter, gogetter. If you're it, hard-charge into editorial offices of AdSalesPerson, the magazine for ad sales persons. Maybe we could have lunch.

AIRCRAFT SALES Top pay, travel, adventure. If you have some fluency in Arabic dialects and happen to own more than one passport, let's talk. Did we say adventure? Silly us, we meant prestige. No adventure. Apply in person to: These Crates Contain Tractor Parts Import-Export Co., not all that far from the airport.

APT. MNGMT. Mature retired couple to live in, spend sunset years dealing with whining and/or abusive tenants at all hours. Write to: Graystark Apartments, Box 13, c/o this paper.

ASTROPHYSICIST The People's Church of the Christmas Cookie has completed construction of the interstellar craft according to the instructions hidden within the dialogue of episode seven of Me and the Chimp. Hundreds of the faithful are in their back

---

wild hotrodders. This is no raceway, but a community of decent Christians. We got the law, we got the rope. You provide the know-how and the hood. You can have the preacher's house; he ain't been no more use than short pants on a pig. Apply in person: Mayor Sweeney Forker, Mystery Hole, Nevada.

CHURCH MUSICIAN Extensive knowledge of Revised Methodist Hymnal req. Send resume and photo of organ to: Rev. Bob, Church of the Suburbs, Shrubland, CA.

COLLECTION You're an experienced field man. You know in your heart that practically every Pontiac, waterbed, or monster speaker set you see deserves to be repoed. If you're our man, you're probably a rat-faced sociopath with a twisted power obsession, and you're ready to move up in a growth industry. We strongly suggest you be in our office at 9:00 AM sharp to avoid further action. The Grabbo Agency, 95 Remit Circle, Unit K.

COUNSELOR Willful and deceitful children from those welfare homes where they breed like rabbits, and not always with benefit of matrimony, either, need firm guidance and a good talking to in the only language they understand, if you know what we mean. Send resume, short essay on discipline to: Bad-Seed House, Box 91, c/o this paper.

DANCERS Sensitive, caring employer. Small, intimate club out-of-the-way location, select clientele. We supply costumes, at first. Apply in person to: Dr. Death, The Pink Mausoleum. It's okay; it's showbiz.

DANCERS If you're 18 or over, how'd you like to make at least a dollar for every hour or year you've been like you are? Hey, no joke. Sensitive,

MUD WRESTLERS No exp. Discreet/respectable. Apply in person: Sonny's Big Wet Entertainment Services, lobby of St. Melvin Residential Hotel. Ask for Sonny. No, wait. First ask for Ernie, then ask for Sonny.

PARAMEDIC Immediate need; man down w/multiple gunshot wounds corner 5th and Oscar. You don't need my name. This has got nothing to do with me.

PARTY CLOWN Seek honest, respectable person of this sort to entertain our little princess and her friends on alternate weekends. This is permanent employment; we'd prefer you were not exposed to a lot of the kind of homes where things can be picked up. We are prepared to negotiate a retainer. Assume simple, non-threatening magic tricks, balloon animals, etc. Send detailed description of costume and brief letter in appropriate tone to: Concierge, Bagsworth Manor, A Neighborhood Otherwise Inaccessible to You, Los Angeles.

RESTROOM ATTENDANT Good with towels? Know your colognes? Like to sneak up on guys in suits at a time when they're not so powerful? This could be for you. Apply in person, obsequiously: Velvet Room, Imbroglio Hotel. Ask for the Captain, and if you want to be traditional, insist on calling him "General."

SALES Are you motivated? A quick learner? Personable?

AUTOMOBILES

you know what I mean. Offer.

ALPHA ROMEO '59 Red, I think. At least, it was. $500 or some furniture.

APHID '56 Rare. Interesting shape. Offer.

ASTON-MARTIN 79 I guess you'd say cute. Offer.

AUSTIN-HEALEY '71 Runs like hell, when it runs. Ask $2000. Take anything.

AUSTIN-HEALEY '59 Classic. Put it together, it's yours.

AUSTIN '59 Hate it. Always hated it. Just take it.

BUICK '85 Cheap Frame not bent. Why do you ask?

BUICK '71 Big. Ugly. No good to anyone.

BUICK '69 Gd. cond. Playboy decal. Offer.

CHEVY '82 Citation. Never driven. Still in box. Offer.

CHEVY '69 Must sell. Scares my cat. Cheap.

CHEVY '58 Original owner still inside. Offer.

CHEVY '57 Cherry. All stock. Original plates. Try and get it.

DESOTO '57 Must sell. Very bad smell from back seat.

DESOTO '49 I know, I'm kidding myself. Offer?

DODGE '71 Boring. Any amount.

FORD '70 Pinto. What the hell, it's transportation. Don't let anybody get behind you, though. Offer.

FORD '67 El Dorado. Custom. One of a kind. $8000 or much lower offer.

FORD '62 Fairlane. Trunk never opened. You be first. Offer.

HONDA '79 Sushi. Gd. cnd. Never driven off a pier and left under mud for three weeks while I raised money for crane. That did not happen. Offer.

JAGUAR '73 $2,500. Also have bear missing a foot and various reptiles. Fuzzy's Small Game Shows, Box 19.

LANCIA '81 Zagato. Hate to part but power windows never worked and air almost gone. $6,000, or first offer.

LINCOLN '81 Town Jester. One owner, grt condition. Eat right, work out daily, get plenty of sleep. Also fantastic wardrobe, right kind of friends, etc. $10,000.

PLYMOUTH '79 Fury. $1,200.

PLYMOUTH '77 Snit. $800. or offer

PLYMOUTH '74 Huff. Offer.

ZEKE '09. Not a car, my grandfather. I need the garage space. Offer.

LOST AND FOUND

LOST wallet, tan cowhide, stuffed with bills. Near person reading book on hypnosis. I don't know, I had it, then I *didn't* have it. It's kind of a blur. Kevin M. P.O. Box 403, this paper.

LOST a … a … watch. Lost a watch. A *gold* watch, very expensive. but it has … *sentimental* value. Really. It belonged to my … *daughter.* That's right. And she died. She died from … from saving her little dog from a fire. And … and she was *rich.* That's why she had the watch. No, wait. I gave her the watch. That's it. It was my watch and I gave it to her and then she died in a fire and I lost it wherever you found it. I've looked everywhere. Charles J. P.O. Box 19, this paper. Really.

AUTOMOTIVE

ALPHA ROMEO '63 Classic, in a sense. Offer.

ALPHA '62 Beyond classic, if

Glib? Can you recognize the OPPORTUNITY OF A LIFETIME when you see it? Were you completely left behind by the computer revolution? Then join our team of young professionals on the ground floor of the WAVE OF THE FUTURE. New World Frog Grooming Accessories, Box RBT, c/o this paper. Don't miss it this time.

SALES Motivated, personable, glib, quick learners wanted! If you have what it takes to play in the big leagues, you belong here! Only *you* limit what you make! Well. We sort of limit what you make. But mostly only you! Sound like what you've been waiting for? Then what are you waiting for? ROGER BILKO SUPER SALES! No address. If you've got what it takes, you'll find us.

SALES Why shouldn't you be getting the big commissions, big cars, big women? Why should they go to the motivated, personable, glib, quick learners? What's happening to this country's values? We approach sales the old-fashioned way: cheap suits, denture breath, relentless high pressure. If you believe it still works, give us a call. The Feh Group, Sherman Bldg., Hackenhackenhack, N.J.

SEA DOGS I not be in need of a crew; but would pass me golden years swappin' tales of the high seas with me old mateys. The grogs be on me. Bring your seabags, just for old times' sake, to: Shanghai Lounge, San Francisco. Hot hors d'oeuvres till lights out. No crew be needed here.

---

caring, happy-go-lucky, hip boss. If you can't have fun, what are you working for? Who's to say what's immoral or illegal or what would gag you just to think about it? You? Me? If you agree with me or would just like to hear more of my philosophy as long as you're naked, hey, get in here. Where? Jeez, I just lost my train of thought. You ever do tha–? I *hate* that. Come on down, we could go on like this all night: Hiney's Zipper Room, where the action's hot and the hat's off the rack and the hoot mon whacka whacka hoo hah.

DANCERS Sensitive, caring boss. Simple club show, legitimate exotic dance. Reasonable hours, pay. Must like animals Ask for Quiet Jimmy, The Beasthole.

DELIVERY I got a double sawbuck for some smart kid who wants to run this shoebox a couple blocks down to Umberto's. That's it. See Itchy, on the corner, white tie. You don't want to look in the box. Trust me on this point.

DOORMAN Exclusive Central Park West apartments. Pref. minimum rap sheet, not too many visible tattoos. We provide tasteful uniform, training. Apply in person: The Flotilla, 1001 W. 86th St. NY, NY.

DRUID Some exp. in arcane rites, human sacrifice, preparation of after-service refreshments. Stonehenge Social Club, Box 7, c/o this paper.

GAME SHOW HOST Articulate, personable young man with some knowledge of small game, esp. badgers, weasels, etc. Some mathematical aptitude pref. Send book or have agent contact: Fuzzy's Small Game Shows, Trail of the Glitzy Pine, Hollywood, Florida.

HANGMAN Small, quiet town near state line is fed up with

That's right! Thousands needed to complete highways abandoned by silly, superstitious natives. All you need is willingness to work and some knowledge of toad god. P.O. Box 13, c/o this paper.

TEACHERS needed in Australia! All subjects, all grades, for no reason, also makes kindergarten to college! No exp. nec., degrees provided on arrival! Send name, your best guess at how to spell BILLY-BONG, and hat size (that's right, you get a hat!) to: We're All Teachers on This Bus, Box 33, Abbo Dabbo Doo, Australia.

EMPLOYMENT OPPORTUNITIES

ACCOUNTANT Absolutely legitimate family-owned business seeks discreet, imaginative, flexible C.P.A. Good benefits, no retirement. See Tulio "No-Fingers" Obligatto, Rebuffo Olive Oil Imports. I cannot recall the exact location at this time.

ACCOUNTS PAYABLE All this time we thought that meant money owed *to* us. Plus who would guess that "credit" meant money *out* and "debit" meant money *in?* We were so proud of 15 years with no debits and no receivables. All we can say is it's a good thing we had no phone. Anyway, we need help now. Apply in person to: Sam and Dave's Financial Planning, 16-B Marca Rosa Drive (behind the Chevron station.)

ACTIVIST Organize rallies, letter placards, steal cityowned bullhorns. No exp. nec. but must be committed enough to refuse payment, should we ever offer it. People's Coalition for Going Limp, Box 341, c/o this tool of the oppressive bourgeois press.

ACTIVITIES COUNSELOR Guide elderly to pool, bath-

---

yards ready to go. Need fuel, someone to steer. Send equations to: Box 666, c/o this scon-to-perish paper.

AUTO MECHANIC Journeyman mechanic needed Car sometimes sort of jerks for no reason, also makes noise something like dragging a small shark through a stovepipe. If you know what it is, send resume and salary history to: Jeff and Sylvia, c/o this paper. I know it's not the generator.

AUTO MECHANIC Remember when all you had to do was pack the differential with sawdust and Ma and Pa Hayseed would plunk down the cash? If you miss the simplicity of the old days, maybe you have some ideas for the eighties. Tell'em to us at: Tubby's Auto-Porium, the dealer with a heart in the heart of South City.

AUTO SALES is every sale a personal vendetta to you? Do you appear unkempt even in a brand-new bright yellow knit suit? Can you remember when you last washed your hair? If not, let's talk. Apply in person to: Tubby's Auto-Porium, the dealer with a heart in the heart of South City.

BAKER Operate newest location Mom's Real Home Made Donuts. No exp. nec. big machine pukes the suckers out as fast as you can ring up sales. Your own chef's hat a plus. Mom's, Unit 412, Tile Forest Mall.

BANKER Privately owned S&L in operation ten years recently discovered we have no president. Somehow just never came up before. Nice paneled office ready and waiting, plus a few things requiring signatures. Please rush resume to: Amicable Savings & Loan, Box 101, c/o this paper.

OUTCALL massage. Sandi.

OUTCALL massage. We go anywhere. Riki.

OUTCALL massage. We do anything. Tiki.

OUTCALL massage. I've seen it all. Believe me. Tavi.

OUTCALL massage. Legitimate massage, trained personnel. Discipline, uniforms. Fred.

SHIATSU massage. Seriously hurts.

SWEDISH massage. Various shrubs employed. Depressing. Ask for Hjürd.

J.C.'S outcall massage. Tough week in town on business? Wheeled and dealed yourself into a few kinks, and just need some medically-trained 18-year-old peachcake to rub your overworked back? Hey, *I* buy it, Bonzo. Who wouldn't? You know the number: 212-BRDS.

VIETNAMESE massage. We have to do something. Nobody wants another restaurant. 415-DONG.

PERSONALS

Bughaffhad, we were happy in our way, were we not? There is much to know. Mulefadda.

Thank you St. Jude. Martin.

Thank you St. Jude. Lewis.

Thank you St. Jude. Buzz.

Thank you St. Jude. Kendall.

Anytime gang. St. Jude.

S. What did you say at the party? I am still under the coats. Let's go home. Naomi.

Burt, come home. I think you have the cat. Priscilla.

SCIENCE IN ACTION
Quiz Page

You must know how it works by now. Review the section and study the illustration to determine whether she is:

A. waiting for a bus.
B. impersonating a bus.
C. smuggling a typewriter.

Section Three

Work
as a Parallel
to Life

Work as a parallel to Life

It has been suggested that work comes closest to making sense when we view it as an allegory of life; that humans at work are in fact acting out a series of parables, or short morality plays, from which the astute observer may extract the philosophical lessons he needs to cope successfully with real life (as opposed to work).

Always eager to give an interesting theory a chance, even if it doesn't happen to be our own (there is no room in science for proprietary jealousy or shallow egotism), let us examine a few of the most venerated institutions of human work in this light, in an objective attempt to determine whether this hare-brained gibberish will hold water.

The Telling of Funny Stories

It seems clear that the most valued quality among office-working humans is the ability to tell funny stories: inevitably, this talent is found to the greatest degree in those of the highest status.

This is demonstrated by the frequency of such exchanges between workers as the following:

"Did you run this proposal by the boss?"
"That clown? Don't make me laugh."
or,
"How the hell did we lose the Balder-dash account?"
"You can thank the joke in the corner office."
and so on.

You see that the correlation is clear; the question is whether there is some moral or lesson which may be drawn from it.

We are forced to conclude that there is, and it finds its expression in an old human adage: *laugh and the world laughs with you, if they want to keep their jobs.*

The parallel-to-life theory wins round one, on points.

34

The Office Party

It is the middle of the afternoon. You are deeply enmeshed in reworking the Balderdash proposal, in a last-ditch effort to save the account. The numbers are complex and the logic slippery, but it is all fresh in your mind because you and your colleagues laboriously hammered it out at lunch. It is a delicate mental structure, ephemeral but complete.

Suddenly your office and your concentration are invaded by the fluttering presence and nasal enunciation of the person whose type is known by many titles in many offices: Den Mother; Queen Bee; Oldest and Most Overly Personal Secretary. She alternately simpers and brays the announcement that your presence is required in Accounting *right now* if not sooner because this is Fran's last day–don't be silly, you must know *Fran,* she's been here almost a *year*–anyway, we're just about to cut the cake and we need your nice baritone–well, to *sing,* of course, silly. And don't you dare be naughty and just mumble, I'll be watching you. And besides, we need a big strong man to open the champagne. I know, aren't I *awful?* But I just snuck in two teensy bottles. She's leaving to get married, after all. Now, you've signed the card, haven't you? Oh, God. Well, you can do it afterward, she won't notice. Now, march! The champagne's under my desk. Your old papers will still be here when you get back.

Your old papers are still there when you get back. But your mental acuity, like Fran, is gone. This is only partly because of the three plastic cups of warm champagne which punctuated the conversation with Fran's fiance, who seemed proud of the clarity of purpose which led him to reveal that he had waited to complete computer repair school before placing the old bun in the oven. The sticky, shapeless mass which was your share of the celebratory cake hunkers malevolently in your wastebasket. Your office smells as if it were recently the scene of an arcane rite involving vanilla extract.

When, after a bit, you become aware that you have been staring at your stapler for over three minutes, you put your coat on, cover the remains of the cake with the remains of the Balderdash account, turn off the lights and leave. Much later, at Grogan's, you realize with a certain furtive satisfaction that you never did sign the card.

The story you have just read, though a dramatization, is by no means imaginary. It is a composite drawn from the accounts of a number of office workers who were asked by us to comment anonymously on the phenomenon of the office party. We believe it to be an accurate representation of their collective experience.

This, then, is the office party. But is the office party life? Let us consider the question dispassionately and scientifically, point by point.

Are your most sincere efforts at productivity usually interrupted by forces beyond your control?

Do you often find yourself in places you don't want to be, with people you don't like, just because you try to be a nice person?

When you fall behind in your work, do you believe that someone else is mostly to blame?

Do you drink to "unwind" because the incompetence of others causes you to feel stress?

Do you sometimes think of ways to get revenge, but only if you could claim it was accidental?

If you answered "yes" to all or even some of these questions, then you would seem, by all accounts, to have a pretty good grip on the workings of real life. In short, we have to admit that the parable theory holds up, at least in this instance: the office party may not be life, but it is a lot like it.

A few types culled from our notebooks, of that sub-phylum most closely associated with the unwanted office party. Genus: Queen Bee

36

The Administrative
Insistent.

The
Overly
Personal
Secretary

The
Goodbye
Girl.

37

39

Is Softball Life?

No institution of human work is more venerated than the company softball team. Surely, therefore, any theory which purports to account for work as a parallel to life must first account for softball. The following paragraphs are an unbiased attempt to do so.

Softball and Truth

Whether or not it is an imitation of life, softball *is* an imitation of another game, which we will call "hardball." This nomenclature leads many initiates to believe that the ball used in "softball" is appreciably softer than the ball used in "hardball." They are disabused of this notion the first time they make a casual bare-handed stop on a hot grounder, but because humans – like anyone else – would rather permanently lose the use of one hand than expose themselves as wimps, no one ever suggests that the game may be misnamed. Thus, a pastime that probably should be known as "unwieldyball," or simply "bighardball," continues unchallenged as "softball," and each succeeding generation is freshly taken in.

It may be stated, then, that softball is based on the tacit perpetuation of a palpable lie: in this it is, so far, not significantly different from life.

Softball vs. Hardball

The hardball is about the size of a hefty peach. It is, and more to the point, it *feels* as if it were consciously designed for the human hand. To grasp a hardball, however casually, is immediately to begin looking around for someone taking a carelessly long lead. The hardball is designed, irresistably, to be thrown.

The softball is larger, as large as an average grapefruit. It does not fit the human hand, but is cunningly designed to come just close enough to create the impression that the awkwardness of its handling is your fault. The only possible grip on the softball leaves the hand not quite open and yet not fully closed, putting one in mind of that type of interrogation cell in which the occupant can neither sit nor stand. The softball is designed, ultimately, to be dropped.

The hardball is unequivocally round, and built to stay that way. The softball starts out similarly, but since it is filled with damp sand (or some equally lively substance) it tends to lose its shape with use. Actually, this would seem to be an advantage, and so it is, at first. It becomes slightly easier to throw as its topography becomes more like that of a burrito than a ball, and it gets (!) softer. So what happens when a softball gets soft? They throw it out, naturally, and bring in a brand new one, freshly hard, dead, subtly oversized, and temporarily round.

The primary object of both hardball and softball, simply stated, is to smack the sucker as far as you can. The successful realization of this objective depends in large part on the physical properties of both bat and ball. A simple comparison test will be useful here: if, having grasped a hardball and finding no suitable target, you throw it with some force toward the ground at your feet, it will come back up with what can only be called dispatch. If you repeat this process with a softball, you may, if you wish, bend and pick it up and repeat the process again. That, however, is it. The softball will not resist, but neither is it going to lift a finger to help.

The bat used in hardball is skinny where you hold it and fat where you hit with it. There are reasons for this. The fat part provides weight and, more important, the magical qualities of ash, an unassuming tree which grows slowly and quietly, producing a certain density of grain which resides at and around the point of contact with the ball, a ball which, as we have already seen, came to *play*. The skinny part, assuming you line up your knuckles and step into it without crowding the plate, provides the *whip* any right-thinking person would want when introducing the edge of the grain to a fastball coming in about letter-high.

That is hardball.

The bat used in softball has less variation in circumference. The softball bat is to the hardball bat as Olive Oyl is to Adrienne Barbeau. You can *miss* with a hardball bat and still at least look all right; if you miss a serious swing with a softball bat, you are likely to pull muscles which you had previously believed to be classified as glands. In terms of psychic and physical satisfaction, getting a hit with a softball bat ranks just below eating low-sodium guacamole.

Life vs. Fun

You probably already know that when someone tells you that you are about to have fun, you are going to experience a snowball dance, a game of charades, or a restaurant where you eat with your hands. These things are not hardball, neither are they life.

When hardball is good it is because neither you nor anyone else has come there for fun. You are there to throw flaming inside fastballs; to drill the put-out throw to home; to taunt and steal the pitcher into nervous collapse; to completely *un-hinge* the second baseman's idle daydream of making the double play; to nail some son of a bitch ten feet off the bag. And so on. These things are hardball.

In softball, you have to pretend that it's fine with you to have a girl at shortstop. Even in hardball, you can forgive the shortstop for dropping an easy blooper. But you will never forget, much less forgive, the spectacle of the shortstop *screaming* at an easy blooper and simultaneously throwing her glove in such a way as to slightly injure the pitcher. This, perhaps more than anything else, is softball.

We could go on, but this seems more than ample demonstration that the parallel-to-life theory simply doesn't fit the facts.

Life is full of heartbreak and bitter disappointment, but it's not nearly as bad as softball.

*Imagine yourself in the situation below in light of the now-discredited theory
that work is a parallel to life. Would you then say that*

A. the doctor has not heard that the theory has been discredited;

B. the doctor *has* heard that the theory has been discredited, but feels
you should be made to understand that one discredited
theory doesn't mean life is a carnival;

C. the doctor has reason to believe you are the person who ran
over his cat some months ago.

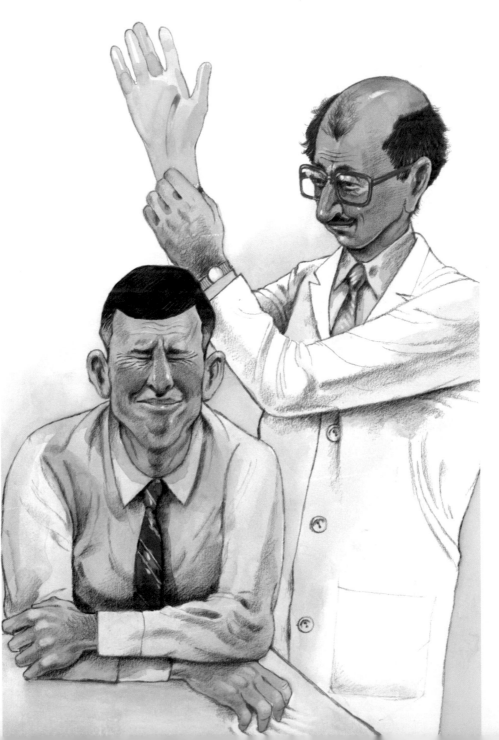

Section Four

The Complete Encyclopedia of Human Work

ACCORDIONIST: A musician who buys only suits with plenty of satin piping.

ACCOUNTANT: Advisor on financial matters, characterized by demeanor of quiet, conservative respectability. Legal resident of Las Vegas.

ACTOR: *See* **WAITER.**

ADMIRAL: Very old sailor, allowed to wear ceremonial hat resembling rear fender of '57 Plymouth.

AGENT: One who is out of the office this week.

AIDE: Naval officer assigned to help the **ADMIRAL** find his hat.

AMBULANCE DRIVER: Always works in teams of two, hence known as "pair o' medics."

ANECDOTIST: *See* **ANESTHETIST.**

ANESTHETIST: One trained in various methods of inducing sleep.

ANNOUNCER: Trained to enunciate difficult phrases, such as, "That's right, Bob, it's a BRAND NEW CAR!"

ANTIQUE DEALER: Extremely aged seller of narcotics.

ANTIQUARIAN: Extremely aged collector of fish.

ARBITRATOR: One sworn to uphold the rights of light-hitting second basemen to be millionaires.

ARCHITECT: Creates new malls.

ARTISAN: Creates new ashtrays.

ARTIST: Creates new systems of investigating the dynamics of spatial relationships while simultaneously stripping away outmoded visual and emotional contexts, resulting in powerful statements which involve the view on a level transcending mere biscuits. *See also* **BIKE MESSENGER.**

ATTENDANT: The one in the corner holding the towels.

ATTORNEY: One who accompanies you into court.

ATTORNEY, FANCY: One who also accompanies you *out* of court.

AUCTIONEER: Appointed to sell off the farm.

AUDITOR: *See* **ATTORNEY,** soon.

AVIATOR: A pilot.

AVIATRIX: A stunt pilot.

BAILIFF: Accompanies you out of court if you are not going same direction as **ATTORNEY.**

BALLADEER: *See* **ACCORDIONIST.**

BANJOIST: *See* **DELIVERANCE.**

BANKER: Stores your money in return for service charge; gives it back to you in return for penalties; loans it to strangers in return for interest. Appoints **AUCTIONEER.**

BARTENDER: Continuously operates large, complicated dishwasher in order to keep beer glasses hot.

BATMAN: Similar to **AIDE,** except **AIDE'S** uniform lacks pointy ears.

Typical Aide   *Typical Batman*

BELLBOY: Instructor of those disoriented by strange hotel rooms, showing them how to find bathroom, open window. Will not leave room until he is satisfied that you have caught on by watching you demonstrate operation of money clip.

BLONDE: Not a job in the strict sense, but included here as often having been the basis for a career.

Accountant in typical dress. At least, typical for our accountant.

Blonde

BOOKKEEPER: Honest and diligent person who keeps careful track of information turned over to accountants.

BOOKSELLER: Honest and diligent person who has kept *copies* of information turned over to accountant and made anonymous arrangement with **DISTRICT ATTORNEY.**

BOUNCER: Assigned to keep undesirables out.

BOUNTY HUNTER: Assigned to bring undesirables in.

C.P.A.: An accountant whose vest matches his suit.

CAB DRIVER: *See* **NOVELIST,** unpublished.

CABIN BOY: *See* **ADMIRAL,** discreetly.

CADDY: Immature **CAD.**

CALL GIRL: *See* **RECEPTIONIST.**

CARDIOLOGIST: A ♥ DR.

CARNY: Transient worker who lives in boxcars and squalid trailers, works long hours for low wages, often required to display himself in degrading circumstances. Refers to rest of population as "marks" or "suckers."

CENSOR: One who ▮▮▮▮▮▮ because he ▮▮▮▮▮ for your own good.

CHAPLAIN: Company cleric.

CHEF: Volatile, non-English-speaking person who carries a large knife and invites taunts by wearing ridiculous hat.

CHICKEN FARMER: Easily frightened agriculturist.

CHIROPRACTOR: A 🦴 DR.

CHOREOGRAPHER: *See* **CHIROPRACTOR**

CHORUS BOY: *See* **CHOREOGRAPHER,** after rehearsal.

CIRCUMNAVIGATOR: Jewish ship's surgeon.

CIVIL SERVANT: Butler who says "Very good, sir," instead of "Whatever you say, Dogbreath."

CLOWN: Person who works with big red nose.

COBBLER: Person who works with big red fingers.

COWBOY: Person who works around cows.

COWPOKE: Person who has worked around cows too long.

DELEGATE: Anyone sent on important mission by others too busy to attend.

DELIVERY PERSON: *See* **DELEGATE.**

DENTIST: One of the few human jobs requiring carefully groomed nose hair.

DEVELOPER: Makes mountains into mall-hills.

DIRT FARMER: Foolish agriculturist who has forgotten to plant anything.

DISK JOCKEY: Person utilizing multi-million dollar broadcast facilities to tell you it's cloudy and the time is 8:27. *See* **WINDOW, CLOCK.**

DISPATCHER: Organizes routes of unpublished novelists.

DRUGGIST: The one in the corner *talking* to the towels.

EDITOR: Person in ~~cluttered~~ *dynamic, eclectic* office who has final control over this description of his ~~job.~~ *profession.*

Cowboy

48

Bookkeeper

Carny (in street clothes)

Cowcoot

Cowdork

49

EDUCATOR: One who can't.

EFFICIENCY EXPERT: One who can't, faster.

ELECTRICIAN: Student of current events. (*See* **HUMORIST** to complain).

ENGINEER: Designer of bridges, towers, tunnels.

ENGRAVER: Designer of twenties, fifties, hundreds.

ENTOMOLOGIST: Proponent of beetlemania.

ENVELOPE STUFFER: Makers of big money at home, even while watching TV.

EQUIPMENT MANAGER: Last one picked.

EXECUTIONER: *See* **ELECTRICIAN.**

EXORCIST: Priest hired to counsel those who lick themselves, others.

FAITH HEALER: Human with great spiritual power, usually situated in the hand, which, when applied with great force to the foreheads of the lame, miraculously causes them to fall over backwards.

FAKIR: Anyone who cannot really do the rope trick.

FASHION MODEL: 19-year-old, 102-pound woman hired to demonstrate appearance of this season's sheer jumpsuits on 53-year-old, 175-pound women.

FILE CLERK: Keeper of records on bastards, etc.

FIRST BASEMAN: Anyone who has never petted below the waist.

FISHERMAN: Irritable person on boat who snaps, "Cast-a-nets!"

FLAMENCO DANCER: Irritable person on table who snaps castanets.

FLAUTIST: One who plays the flaut.

FLOORWALKER: Prostitute who works indoor malls.

FLORIST: One who play the flor.

FLYBOY: *See* **CHORUS BOY.**

FOLK SINGER: Sings proletarian songs to accompaniment of $35,000.00 custom-made guitar.

FOOTMAN: Specialist to whom **CHIROPRACTOR** sends you for second opinion.

FURRIER: A condition; not a job.

GAME WARDEN: Prison administrator willing to cut cards for your sentence, double or nothing.

GAS STATION ATTENDANT: Inhabitant of tiny booth whose native language contains no words for "air," "water," or "restroom."

GAFFER: Fourth from the final credit, usually falling between "Assistant to Mr. Redford," and "Best Boy."

GASTRONOMIST: Scientist who generally has the observatory to himself.

GIGOLO: Overweight jackhammer operator.

GLAZIER: Person responsible for the final stages of donut manufacture.

GRIP: Person who holds things for the **GAFFER.**

GUITARIST: Person assigned to ensure that you keep your eyes on your plate in Mexican restaurants.

Gigolo   *Educator*

HABERDASHER: Member of the Olympic track team from the tiny nation of Haber, no longer extant. Most of the team has gone into the clothing business.

HARPIST: Popular historian specializing in Marx Brothers movies.

HAWKER: Salesman of pharmaceuticals, especially expectorants.

HERBALIST: Popular historian specializing in Brazil '66 recordings.

HOD CARRIER: Anyone infected with the hod virus.

HOOFER: See COWHAND.

HOUSEBOY: Domestic pest common to warm climates, as Beverly Hills.

HOUSE DETECTIVE: Person you call if you want your house followed.

HOUSEKEEPER: See BANKER.

HUMORIST: This is not a job. The sad thing is they're *proud* of that.

HYPNOTIST: A charlatan *buk-buk* who falsely claims *buk-buk* to be able to modify your behavior *buk-buk-baGAWK* without your knowing it.

ICHTHYOLOGIST: Scientist who finds the feel of dead fish distasteful, and doesn't mind saying so.

ICEMAN: Grown man who constantly sticks out his tongs.

ICON ASSEMBLERS: Workers who, in system, are able to produce as many as 4500 True Crosses in an eight-hour period. *(See overleaf.)*

IDEA MAN: Okay, listen. First we have this cheap rip-off of Disneyland in a family pizza place where a salad costs maybe six bucks but we give change in tokens that *only* work in the video machines which *we own*. Only we don't *tell* anybody about that part until they've stood in line for twenty minutes under a strobe light. Is the public gonna love this, or what? And wait'll you hear the great name we got for the mouse.

IDIOT SAVANT: Stupid butler, maid, etc.

IDIOMATIC: Mechanical version of stupid butler, maid, etc.

ILLUSTRATOR: Draws pictures for a paycheck.

IMMUNOLOGIST: Draws blood for a paycheck.

INCUMBENT: Draws paychecks.

IMPORTER: Shops the world to bring in a variety of cute figurines and adorable stuffed animals, all heavier than they look, for some reason.

INDENTURED SERVANT: *Old* butler, maid, etc.

INDIAN AGENT: Off the reservation this week, but he'll get back to you.

INDIAN CLUB: Bar which has been declared off limits to cavalrymen.

INFIELDER: One of those four millionaires out there holding their crotches and spitting on their shoes.

INFILTRATOR: The man who cleans the pool.

INSPECTOR: Person who puts little numbers in your shorts.

INSPECTOR GENERAL: Person who puts little numbers in anything.

INTERN: Young, inexperienced person who is kept awake for four days straight and then told to decide whether or not that leg of yours should come off. Harmless hazing which gives other doctors a laugh.

INVERSION THERAPIST: Advocate of the idea that hanging upside down until you black out is good for you, and that people will pay to be instructed in this practice. (EDITOR'S NOTE: It's obvious that they're pulling our legs, but we left this in anyway. Humans are great kidders when you get to know them, though of course they consistently over-estimate our gullibility. You should hear the one they tried on us about shaving with two blades at once. At bottom, they are a simple, fun-loving people.)

INVESTMENT COUNSELOR: Jack London told the story of the Swede who, during the Gold Rush, discovered that he could stay warm and dry *and* make a fortune by building boats for prospectors who were travelling far into the frozen Yukon in search of gold. Most failed to find it, of course, and many never came back. All investment counselors are familiar with this story.

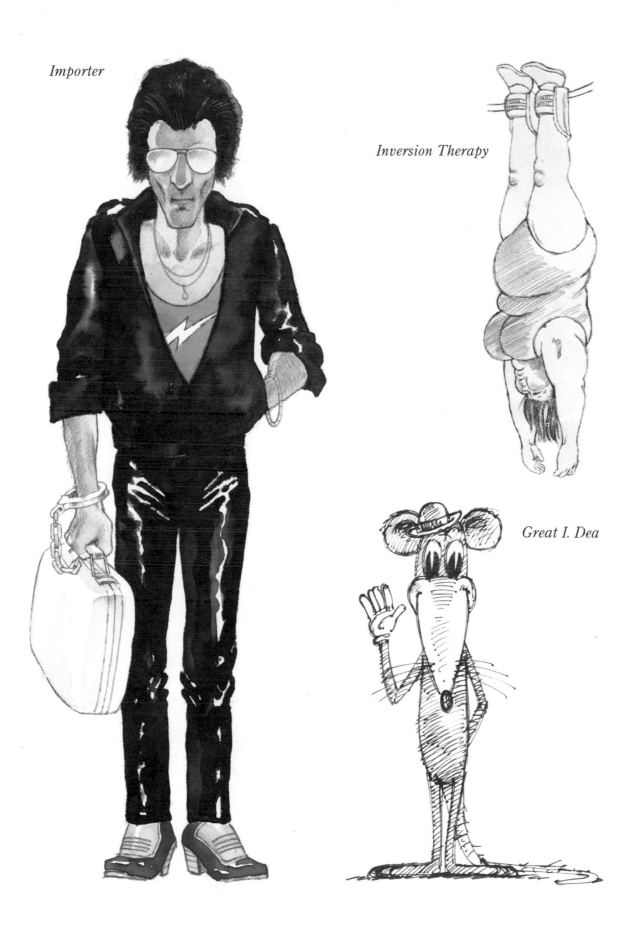

Importer

Inversion Therapy

Great I. Dea

The Group Four Icon Assemblers day shift, Musical Mantel Molds Division of Hugeco Industries, with Line Supervisor Otto "Ham" Elder.

JAGUAR SALESMAN: Will throw in 100 lbs. of kibble if you can see your way clear to write a check today.

JAPANESE GARDENER: The only person in your household who understands the VCR.

JAYWALKER: Retired person willing to exercise your bird.

JET PILOT: What the recruiting sergeant says you will be shortly after basic training. *See* **COOK.**

JOCKEY: Small persons hired to protect expensive saddles from mud damage.

JOURNALIST: Can you say, "Jackie to Wed Psychic; Aliens Capture Bigfoot?" You may be a journalist.

KAKAPO: A nocturnal burrowing New Zealand parrot, or possibly a typo. In any case, it's not a job.

KEYNESIAN: Unemployed economist.

KILN OPERATOR: The person who must break the news that your ashtray exploded.

KIN: Person who can get you into the union. *See* **UNCLE GINO.**

KISS: A common business acronym, standing for "Keep Stupid." No, it must be "Keep It, Stupid." No, that can't be right. But close enough.

KIT: What the press is given when the star doesn't feel like talking.

KO-KO: *See* **PO-PO.**

LAB BOYS: Criminologists generally much older than their title implies. *See* **DRAGNET.**

LACKADAISICAL: A florist with limited selection.

LADDER SALESMAN: Ask him how sales are so he can say, "Oh, we've rung up a few."

LANDLORD: Mythical god of the apartment.

LANCER: Boil unmaker.

LIBRARIAN: Person who patiently explains that the rules clearly state that no medical reference books may leave the building under any circumstances, and, in any case, owning a stethoscope does not prove that you are a doctor. Especially a stethoscope made of yellow plastic.

LIEUTENANT: *See* **SERGEANT,** if you really want anything done.

LIGHT MAN: The one in the corner snapping the switches.

LINGUIST: Italian prep chef.

LOCKER ROOM ATTENDANT: The one in the corner snapping the towels.

MALE MODEL: *See* **TANNING SALON.**

MANUAL LABORER: Agricultural worker, often in country illegally. *See* **ALFONSO; JOSE LABORER.**

MARATHONER: Person who derives great personal satisfaction from an experience very similar to breathing into a plastic bag for about thirty minutes. Why doesn't he just do that? Starve *your* brain of oxygen for a few months and then see if it occurs to you.

MARINE BIOLOGIST: Member of elite corps of scientists, always first to hit the tidepools.

MEAT INSPECTOR: Person who sees to it that your paté contains no more mouse droppings and roach legs than the government says is good for you.

MOOSE HUNTER: A **MASON** with a gun.

MOVER: *See* **SHAKER.**

MORTICIAN: Takes pale, slovenly dead people and makes them look natural by giving them a tux and a tan.

MUDDER: A racehorse which has recently foaled.

MUSHROOM SORTER: Picks out the good parts, leaving only stems etc. behind.

MUSICIAN: Ditto.

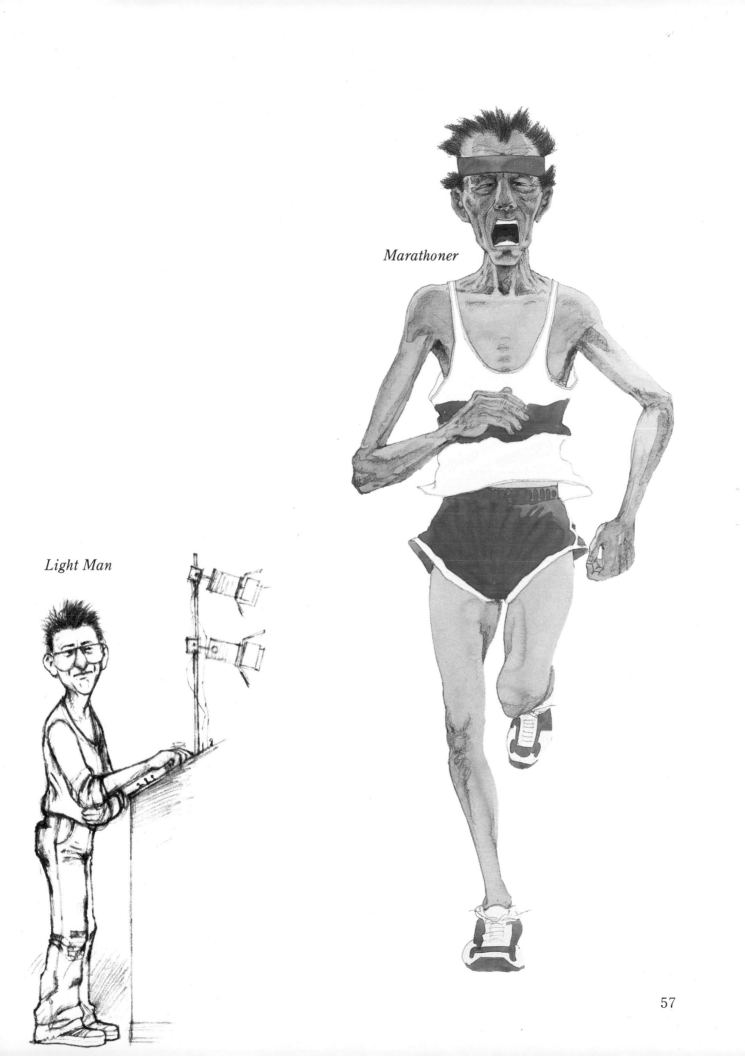

Marathoner

Light Man

NARK: Large predatory fish with a speech impediment. *See* **MARRICUDA.**

NASH SALESMAN: A follower of the Kaiser.

NE'ER-DO-WELL: Hired hand whose duties do not include polishing the pump handle.

NEPOTIST: Hypnotist's sister's son, looking for a job.

NETWORK EXECUTIVE: Thinks there's a fresh new series in the above idea if you make the hypnotist a divorced mother and add a little kid who makes double-entendre wisecracks. Could be called *Snap Out Of It,* though that's just off the top of his head.

NIGHT CLERK: Despite such acute hearing that he can identify a bill's denomination by its crinkle, he never seems to catch a name.

OARSMAN: The only person in the dinghy who needs to see where they're going, yet faces backwards.

OBSTETRICIAN: Brings people into the world against their will.

OCCULTIST: *See* **OBSTETRICIAN.**

OPTIMIST: If an optimist and a pessimist were on a sinking ship, the pessimist would say that they were all going to die. The optimist would say that, yes, they were all going to die, but it takes time for a ship to sink and his drink is still half full.

ORACLE: Frozen public speaker on a stick.

ORGAN GRINDER: *See* **PATÉ CHEF.**

PALINDROMIST: Writer who goes both ways.

PALINDROMIST, OBESE: Not a tub, but a ton.

PASTE-UP ARTIST: *See* **ACK**

PAVLOVIAN: Behavioral research scientist identifiable by the sign on his door: "Please knock; bell works."

PERSONAL SECRETARY: Office worker with an advanced degree in English Literature, the better to make nice clean photocopies and legible mailing labels.

PLAINSMAN: Ugly settler.

PLENIPOTENTIARY: A prison where you get a lot to eat.

PROFESSOR: *See* **CURVE** or see **COUNSELOR** for transfer.

PUBCRAWLER: Person who knows the shortest distance between two pints.

PUMA HUNTER: *See* **COUGAR VICTIM.**

Personal Secretary

Professor

QUANTUM MECHANIC: Person who greases the big telescope.

QUARTET: More than a pint; less than a quart.

QUEEN: Usually characterized by regal and gracious presence; sumptuous flowing gowns. Can do things with gaffer's tape that would amaze you.

QUICHE CHEF: Gesundheit.

QUICK STUDY: *See* **DEAN** for new counselor.

QUISLING: Young, untrustworthy waterfowl.

QUORUM: Four big guys who agree with you.

RABELAISIAN SCHOLAR: Student of the classics with gargantuan curiosity.

RACKETEER: Person whose olive oil business is a front for a string of tennis courts.

RACONTEUR: Person whose olive oil business is a front for a string of French restaurants.

RAG AND BONE MAN: Chiropractor who also owns a chain of clothing stores.

REALTOR: Person who doggedly refuses to accept the fact that his job title has only two syllables. *See* **REALATOR.**

RELATIVIST: Mathematician who claims to be a distant cousin of Einstein.

RESIDENT: Pen-pal for discount stereo and furniture stores.

RESERVIST: An unusually shy military officer.

RUGBY PLAYER: Person who knows at least forty different drinking games and filthy lyrics to at least nine pop standard tunes. None of this is a job, but no one seems to have the heart to tell him.

SALESMAN: Person whose livelihood depends on his ability to do complex mental calculations, since a bad run of liar's dice can wipe out a month's commissions.

SALES TRAINEE: Salesman who does not yet have his name on a dice cup.

SALESWOMAN: Person who has no intention of being denied, on the basis of her sex, the right to slam dice cups, grope waitresses, and trade witticisms about flatulence and genitalia. (See overleaf.)

SECURITY GUARD: Person who discourages potential thieves by giving the impression that your place of business is occupied by a Paramount usher with a gun.

SELF-HELP AUTHOR: Anyone who has figured out that not only is it *okay* to be a self-serving jerk, you can make a living at it.

SENTRY: Member of armed forces receiving valuable training for civilian life. *See* **SECURITY GUARD.**

SETTLER: Pioneer farmer whose home was a sod hut.

SOD-BUSTER: Small cordless vacuum cleaner used by **SETTLER.**

SODA JERK: Summer job held by young future **SELF-HELP AUTHOR.**

SONG AND DANCE MAN: *See* **ACCOUNTS PAYABLE CLERK.**

Rugby Player

Security Guard

Women in sales.

Despite the disadvantage of her well-known lack of mathematical aptitude, this new sales trainee assured us that she was determined to overcome these noxious, outmoded male bastions. At least, we think that was the word. It was a little loud in there.

TAB INSTALLER: Person who inserts the little sharp thing in the seams of shirts, somewhere in the neck area.

TACKLE: Professional athlete who likes people, in the same sense that Oscar Mayer likes pigs.

TAILOR: *See* **TALK SHOW**

TALK SHOW HOST: Person willing to engage in conversation with grown men named "Shecky."

TARPON: Member of a painting crew responsible for covering the furniture.

TENET: A common misspelling; *see* **LANDLARD**

TOAD GOD: Primitive deity whose demands included after-service refreshments of coffee, punch, and flies.

TRAPPIST: Monk of a particular religious order, noted for their stories of agnostics who have gnawed their own legs off to escape.

TRUCK DRIVER: Oddly over-zealous humans who will fire up a 300-horsepower diesel and drive through three states just for a cup of coffee. It could be those little white pills.

TUPPERWARE DESIGNER: Confident worker who knows that if he designs a container for keeping fish eyes, you'll buy it because your best friend's aunt is selling it in your living room.

U-BOAT CAPTAIN: Hans across the sea.

ULTERIOR DECORATOR: Has secret reasons of his own for doing your apartment over.

UNDERDOG: The one who will later take care of the pups.

UNDERTAKER: The last person to dress you funny.

UNDERSEA DEMOLITION ENGINEER: Gets rid of useless office buildings, shopping centers, etc. which have foolishly been built underwater.

UNION ORGANIZER: Idealist who fights unfair employment practices with every means at his disposal, including vandalism, extortion, and assault.

UNICYCLIST: Bike rider who dresses like a girl, or vice versa.

UROLOGIST: They caught the proctologist, so you thought it was safe to go back in the medical building.

USED CAR SALESMAN: Person suffering from an unreasonable fear of adding figures in a vertical column and arriving at a total.

USHER: Person assigned to see to it that friends of the groom make it to the parking lot before they throw up.

VALET: The flat area between two *montes*. (we realize that many of these are not jobs at all, but a little general knowledge certainly isn't going to hurt you.)

VANGUARD: The one who stays to watch the truck while the others go get the piano.

VARMINT: A rat-flavored breath freshener, no longer on the market.

VATMAN: Pumps the synthetic ethanol into the Table Red, but never before it's time.

VEGETARIAN FEMINIST: We are, she believes, what we eat. In her book, that makes you dead meat.

VELCRO SALESMAN: Once he gets started, just talks fastener and fastener.

VENDOR: The leader of a race of alien robots from space who disguise themselves as soft drink dispensers in order to infiltrate our civilization. They have been among us for years. Soon they will strike, and all earthlings will be their helpless slaves.

VENOM COLLECTOR: Despite its reputation, the hardest part of this job is finding a low enough milking stool.

VERMIN: *See* **FURRIER.**

VISIONARY: Now try the third line again, please, this time with your left eye.

VITAMIN SALESMAN: Well-preserved evangelical person who speaks persuasively and very slowly, so as not to wobble his neck.

VIXEN: Daughter of a president.

VOCALIST: Any description of laundry; grocery items, etc. which is not written down.

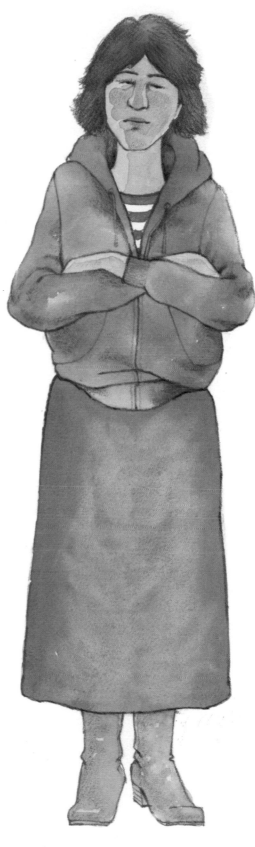

Vegetarian Feminist

WABBI: Elmer Fudd's religious advisor. See **PWIEST.**

WAITER: Service person who dresses like a mortician, but does not give the impression that he thinks you look natural.

WAREHOUSEMAN: Expert in systematic storage, even able to read inverted stock numbers, as in: FRAGILE! THIS SIDE UP.

WASHERWOMAN: Female clerk in plumbing supply store.

WASTE MANAGEMENT ENGINEER: An industrial optimist who believes that sooner or later they'll find a use for all this stuff, and when they do he'll be in on the ground floor.

WASTREL: Profligate member of traveling blackface banjo troupe.

WOMEN, DEAN OF: Motto behind her desk reads, "Discipline doesn't need a reason."

WORD PROCESSOR: Operator of a machine by the same name which has revolutionized the field of writing by making it possible, at the touch of a key, to erase an entire novel.

WORDSMITH: A writer checking into a motel with his research assistant.

WORM FARMER: Highly efficient tiller of the soil who is able to continue working even if cut in half.

XENOPHOBE: A neurotic from another planet.

XMAS TREE FARMER: Person who will not only allow you to persecute the tree of your choice, but will then nail it to a wooden cross for you.

X-RAY TECHNICIAN: This person's *real* job is to convince you that the lead-lined bib is perfectly adequate protection, and the only reason he leaves the room is that the switch happens to be out there, for no good reason.

YAK HERDER: Takes large, hairy items to market.

YAM GROWER: Same as **YAK HERDER,** except makes a better living because, due to the lack of anything like the Yam Growers' Association, candied yak has never caught on.

YEARBOOK EDITOR: The one whose picture appears on pp. 9, 14, 23, 25, 27, 29, 36, 40, 44, 63, 67, 68, 82, 105, 107, and 119, none of which make him look stupid.

YO-YO DEMONSTRATOR: Sylvester Stallone's voice coach.

ZARATHUSTRA: *(Arch.)* A public spaker.

ZEN BUDDHIST: What is the sound of one hand clapping? It sounds to us like closing out of town.

ZERO PILOT: Every airline gives prospective pilots an intelligence and aptitude test. Somebody has to come in last.

ZIPPER INSPECTOR: A childish ploy to cop a feel; not a job. (Though it is available as a major course of study at San Diego State.)

ZOOKEEPER: The lion is Simba; the gorilla is Bwana. Meet the guy who feeds them, Lefty.

ZOOLOGY MAJOR: She thought it sounded cuddlier than The Humanities.

ZORRO: Mexican loyalist who named himself for a small, crafty canine. Had a little-known cousin in the same business. *See* **THE MARK OF PERRO.**

Zoology Major

Dean of Women

Quiz Page

The Encyclopedia of Work is the result of massive and painstaking research by dedicated scientists, many of whom took time off from their day jobs, and we believe the quiz which follows it should reflect something of its dignity and scope. Anyway, you've had it entirely too easy up to now.

Two-Part Essay Question.
Part I.

Trace the development of work from the early clam standard to the inception of the employee lounge. Using DaBinkey's *Remembrance of Foretellings* as a reference, explain the three inter-related concepts which were to be the foundation of his writings, but which he lost somewhere downtown.

Part II.

Describe the influence of work on the human language. Include, but do not limit yourself to, such examples as, "No, I think I can definitely say those are not my initials," and, "Aren't you overreacting to refer to a simple compliment or two as 'harassment?'" Give two possible reasons for the failure of any personnel manager ever to see any irony in the concept of the "mental health day."

You have one hour to complete your essay in the space provided below. Have a friend or relative who owns or is able to borrow a watch keep time, and remember that if you have not yet paid for this book you would do well to work lightly in pencil.

_____

_____

_____

_____

_____

_____

_____

_____

_____

_____

_____

Section Five

The Dawn
of Work

Crude beginnings.

How did work as we know it begin? What natural and social forces shaped it into the forms we recognize today? When was the first personal day? The answers to these and other work-related questions, believed to be forever obscured by the mists of time, have recently come to light through a series of startling finds near what is now the Motown Heights Mall ("More than just a shopping

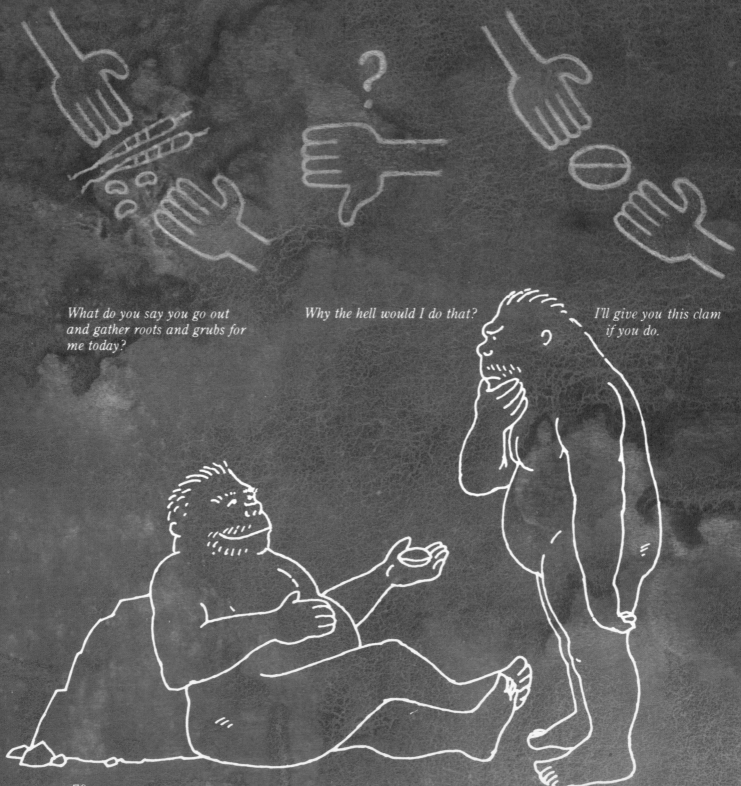

What do you say you go out and gather roots and grubs for me today?

Why the hell would I do that?

I'll give you this clam if you do.

70

center") near Detroit.
The most significant of these discoveries, without doubt, is the cave painting reproduced below. After painstaking translation of the primitive (yet eerily, unmistakably human) pictographs, archaeologists now agree that what is recorded on this ancient rock wall is nothing less than the actual invention of work.

Make it two clams.   *You drive a shrewd and difficult bargain, but okay.*   *When do I start?*

Two firsts.

This cave painting (above), found not so very far from the one reproduced on the previous pages, was unaccompanied by pictographs, rendering it virtually impossible for modern scientists to interpret with any degree of certainty. One school of thought maintains that it is the first comic strip, but this idea has been largely discredited since a careful search of nearby artifacts has failed to turn up a single doll, greeting card, or calendar featuring the same characters.

Once the idea of work was established, various rates of exchange were probably arrived at by simple trial and error, as in this artist's conception (right). How they communicated the exact nature of the work to be performed remains a mystery, although we have another artist's conception of that. We wish you could see it, but unfortunately we lacked the space to print it, or so our editor says. Seems to us there would have been plenty of room right here.

What they did before there was work.

From the vantage point of this enlightened time, it is difficult indeed to imagine the dreariness of human life prior to the invention of work, every day stretching before them like a vast, featureless desert, hour after empty hour. Even the gathering of food, often cited as an example of something to do, seems to be greatly overrated when we remember that we are talking about a time *before* the invention of farming. If the season happened to bring an unusually good crop of roots and grubs, making food plentiful and easy to get, there was no one whose responsibility it was to burn or bury the surplus. Clearly, the acquisition of food under such conditions could not have taken all that much of the poor pre-work human's time.

The vicious cycle created by plentiful free food is only one example of the generally miserable conditions of this era of human history, yet it seems only morbidly depressing to continue. Suffice it to say that before work there was chaos, and let us move on to more uplifting considerations.

The entire question of what humans did before there was work may never be answered completely, since record-keeping is, of course, work. Many scholars, however, seem confident that no one is likely to prove them wrong when they assert that the pre-work human probably whiled away the hours with such activities, besides the already-discussed foodgathering (Fig. 1), as primitive group entertainment (Fig. 2), and occasional physical competitions (Fig. 3).

Fig. 1

Fig. 2

Fig. 3

After the big one.

Interestingly, certain pre-work activities bear a superficial resemblance to modern human life. Of course, there is no real connection, and it seems certain that the primitive and simple humans (shown engaging in an unusually ambitious food-gathering session) were incapable of feeling anything like the sense of accomplishment and satisfaction the modern human feels at having done something truly useful.

The example in the inset below, for instance, shows a group of work-fulfilled modern humans in the process of landing the Red Top Camper Shell account, through a combination of a professionally prepared presentation and some truly inspired sucking around. Their justifiable pride at bringing home the big one is unmistakable.

The brain, then and now.

In order to diagram the essential differences between the modern and the pre-work human brain, we have created this artist's conception of the brain itself, shown here as if it could just sort of float outside your skull. Of course, we have greatly simplified the whole thing for the purpose of demonstration. If you took a *real* brain out of a skull, no amount of tape or anything like that could get it to hold its shape this way. This is because the brain, as you probably know, has no bones. The whole slimy gray mass would simply collapse on itself, slopping over your tray or petri dish or whatever you were trying to carry it in, and at the very least you could kiss your suede shoes goodbye. Not to mention your lunch.

Still, there's no getting around it. This is what the most important organ in your body looks like, and without the efforts of innumerable research scientists who, over the years, have been willing to handle and even *slice up* actual

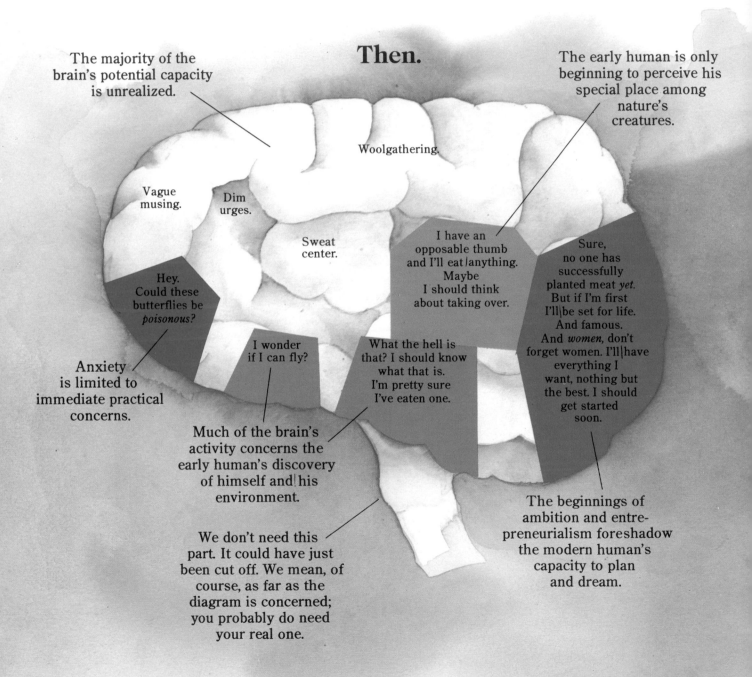

Then.

The majority of the brain's potential capacity is unrealized.

The early human is only beginning to perceive his special place among nature's creatures.

Woolgathering.

Vague musing.

Dim urges.

Sweat center.

I have an opposable thumb and I'll eat anything. Maybe I should think about taking over.

Sure, no one has successfully planted meat *yet*. But if I'm first I'll be set for life. And famous. And *women,* don't forget women. I'll have everything I want, nothing but the best. I should get started soon.

Hey. Could these butterflies be *poisonous?*

Anxiety is limited to immediate practical concerns.

I wonder if I can fly?

What the hell is that? I should know what that is. I'm pretty sure I've eaten one.

Much of the brain's activity concerns the early human's discovery of himself and his environment.

We don't need this part. It could have just been cut off. We mean, of course, as far as the diagram is concerned; you probably do need your real one.

The beginnings of ambition and entre-preneurialism foreshadow the modern human's capacity to plan and dream.

brains no matter how much it creeped them out, we might still know very little about its inner workings.

(By the way, we cannot really recommend that you try any of this at home, since it requires years of intensive training as well as a good deli-style meat slicer, something not found in the average kitchen. But if you're determined, be sure to wear old clothes.)

As you can see, the effect that the invention of work has had on the human brain over the centuries has been significant. Not only have individual processes become more complex and sophisticated, but much more has been physically called into play, shown by the color-coded areas of the diagram. Where once as much as 70% of the brain was wasted on more or less just thinking about things, the modern human finds that holding a job accounts for pretty much his entire cranial capacity.

Now.

Red tie/blue suit. Or is it blue tie/red suit?

Would it be too much to marinate my socks in Paco Rabanne?

Someday the bastard will walk in here when I haven't just put my feet up.

What ever possessed me to put that in a *memo*? If I see her anywhere *near* the Xerox machine, I might as well dust off the old resumé.

Cough center.

Speech center.

Shopping center.

They've got a 256K hard disk for the same price, but our 128 has a graphics board that lights up like Caesar's Palace. We'll rip their balls off in the high school market.

Is Club Med still cool? Do they get you on the beads? Do you have to be in the tug-o'-war? Research.

So an out-of-town client needs a date for dinner. That doesn't exactly make me a *pimp*, does it?

If *he* gets carpet, *I* get carpet, or I walk. It's the principle of the thing.

Should I buy the Playboy binder, or continue casual scattering on the end tables? Should I *have* end tables?

What was simple impulse in the early human is now automatically screened for logic and rationality.

Work is more than merely a livelihood, having become infused with a spirit of friendly competition.

Primitive simplistic ambition has become a complex inter-related system for self-advancement.

Quiz Page

There are several theories regarding the exact division between the pre-work human and the earliest true modern man. Which theory is best illustrated in this artist's conception?

A. Standing up straight instead of slouching unattractively.

B. Giving serious thought to a diet higher in roots, lower in grubs.

C. First actual use of toolbelts.

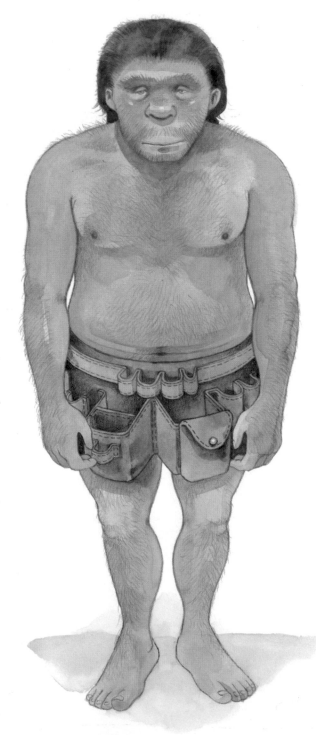

Section Six

Getting to Work

The Age of DaBinkey.

Between the extremes of the dark pre-work era and modern human life, where the question, "What do you do?" is laden with ritualistic meaning, lie the tumultuous middle years. This period marks the beginning of the human struggle to refine the pursuit and practice of work to its current high level of stylization.

To appreciate the enormity of this undertaking, it is necessary to understand that even the theory or work was still in its infancy, and its practice was, at best, simplistic. Such sublime refinements as the sports analyst, the consumer advocate, and the color consultant still lay far in the future. At this time, everyone who worked at all either *made* something, *grew* something, *killed* something, or was a priest.

While this early tendency toward specialization, dividing workers into tinkers, farmers, knights, and priests, was clearly on the right track, two significant limitations prevented any real further progress: there still wasn't that much to do, and they were all jobs which could be done at home. So while the middle-period human had at least the beginnings of work, he knew nothing of the concept of *getting to work*.

However, every age produces its visionaries, though they are not always recognized as such in their own times. One such man was Leo DaBinkey, a tinker's son who (ironically, considering his eventual impact on the development of work) never actually did a day's work in his life. Further, his hare-brained inventions and crackpot speculations, all written down in a "code" so transparent that a child could have deciphered it, made him an object of derision among his contemporaries, who appear to have tolerated him primarily because of his willingness to run small errands and clean up around the great libraries and universities in which they gathered.

DaBinkey hit on at least one idea, however, that overshadowed all his other silliness and assured him an honored place among the great thinkers of history. Tragically, however, this was not known until long after his untimely death, the result of repeated cuffings by the intellectuals whose simple errands he invariably screwed up.

What he said was this:

"What is the life of a man, though he work as tinker or priest, but that, his work being well known to him, and also his home, that anon all is sameness? And what is the soul of a man, though he be farmer or knight, that sameness is not a vexation of the spirit? Does not the farmer barter the goat? Does not the knight require the newly vigorous steed? Does not the tinker from time to time request of his wife that she wear the wig? So it is over our land, and over our hearts, and our minds. The times and the people are not in accord with me, yet I say there should be more than four jobs, and we should not work at home, rather should we have many jobs, only live afar, and all try to get there at the same time."

…live afar, and all try to get there at the same time.

With those words, Leo DaBinkey single-handedly moved work out of the middle ages and into the modern world, a contribution to his fellow man so significant that most scholars are inclined to forgive his other major predictions, even including the one about civilization eventually abandoning the wheel in favor of specially-bred weasels somehow affixed to the feet.

DaBinkey made copious notes of practically his every idle thought, in the supremely silly belief that they were indecipherable by anyone but himself. Actually, their secrecy was assured by the fact that no one was remotely interested but himself.

Public transportation.

One of the many contemporary variations of DaBinkey's Law: a group of modern young women, all

NO PARKING

either on their way to work, on their way home from work, or, in some cases, out looking for work.

Walking to work.

The near-universality of DaBinkey's Law notwithstanding, many urban humans still prefer the simple pleasure of walking to work. This affords them a chance to breathe the morning air, take some mild but healthful exercise, and exchange an occasional pleasantry or two with fellow workers before confining themselves to their offices for the day.

In this way, the modern urban human combines certain advantages usually associated with the country – such as the warmth of contact with other humans – with the greater security and convenience of life in the city.

Which well-known phrase from the writings of DaBinkey is most applicable to the illustration?

A. "...therefore say not arrive when you will; say rather arrive at an hour most Godawful, that no man may regard it clear-eyed and so think, 'why go?'"

B. "If on fire, especially of the clothing, running avails not. Either disrobe or roll in fresh dung, whichever least embarrasseth."

C. "When visiting the wife of another, know much of his work, which knowledge avails thee two-fold: either speak to her of that which is familiar, if speaking be necessary; or, more to the point, remember what time he gets home."

Section Seven

The Hidden Purpose of Talking About Work

Talking about work while at work but on a break.

The attentive reader will by now begin to understand that ritual behavior, however pointless it may appear to the outsider, always has a disguised usefulness. What sets the human behavior apart, as the following examples will demonstrate, is the unusual effectiveness of the disguise.

One of the difficulties arising from modern specialization is that many humans have become unfamiliar with the details of their fellow humans' work. This has led in turn to the proliferation of certain socially disruptive ideas. It is not difficult, for instance, to find humans who seem to believe that just because you call for a taxi at a certain time, or ask clearly for wine with the appetizer, or simply say aloud that you would like to buy the ball-peen hammer in the window display, these things should then just *happen*, as if by magic.

These are attitudes born of ignorance, and it is clear that they must be corrected if humans engaged in widely disparate areas of work are to continue in harmonious co-existence. This is the important purpose being served by the seemingly irrelevant act of talking about work while at work.

Though these conversations are conducted as if they were casual–even, among the more expert practitioners, banal–they are actually designed to edify the uninformed outsider as to the stringent demands, stressful conditions, and totally gross stuff like department managers who have total *cows* if you go like *one minute* over your break, or if your sales tickets and register tapes don't match *totally* to the penny. Like I'm sure Macys is going to go totally *broke* or something.

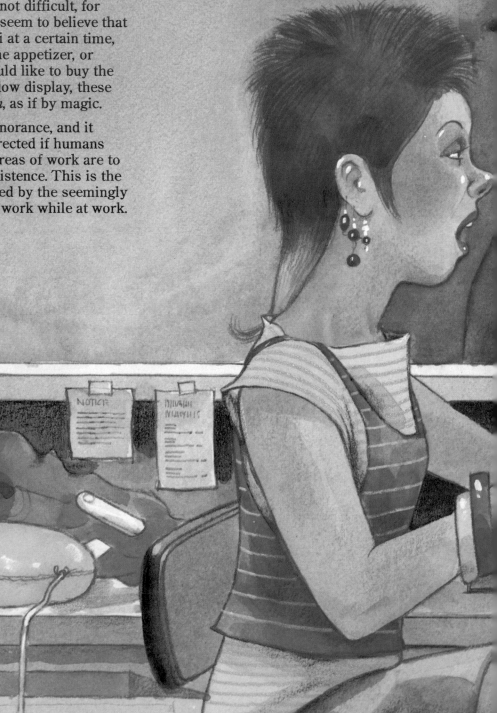

Talking about work while at home having a few brewskis.

One of the most interesting aspects of such stylized behavior as work is that it becomes, over the generations, so second-nature to its participants as to give the impartial observer the impression of something like telepathy. A notable example of this is the common interaction between workers and their supervisors, especially among those workers given to the wearing of compartmented toolbelts and really big clip-on tape measures (obvious vestigial warrior accoutrements).

In this case, there is little mystery about the true purpose of their behavior—the supervisor is protecting the worker from being stripped of his toolbelt, and the subordinate is sparing his superior the embarrassment of being shown up as a pusillanimous windbag hiding behind hollow authority. These are, after all, mature adults, and no other explanation seems plausible. The wonder is the unfailing accuracy of their timing: the supervisor always stops his harassment, according to the worker's own report, just *one word short* of collecting a knuckle sandwich, and the subordinate will engage his superior in one of these confrontations only at a time when *no fellow worker will happen by* to witness it.

Laudable behavior, of course. But how do they know?

Talking about work while at the club.

This behavior takes place almost exclusively at the very highest levels of human work, where the act of talking about work has become indistinguishable from the work itself. Again, there is a subtle purpose being served by the seemingly gratuitous removal of the process from the workplace. To understand this, imagine yourself in an office, surrounded by sophisticated means of communication and dedicated underlings, ready to spring to put your plans into action. How easy it would be to say such things as, "Since we all agree it seems a good idea, let's get on with it,"

or, "Why don't we just pop into accounting and cut that check right now?" Very soon you would find yourself completing projects right and left until there was nothing but for everyone to go home.

Such a return to the dark ages is forestalled, in part, by moving the action to places which were never designed for work at all, and sticking to them. In such environments, talking about work is more along the lines of, "I think you have a point there, Fahrquahrt. Memo me on that for the Tuesday breakfast meeting, why don't you," or, "I

think we should pursue this line of thought with the marketing boys at racquetball." In this way, the consideration of actually doing something is put into a sort of permanent holding pattern until it simply goes away. This is central to the very spirit of high-level work, where it is well known that the only sure way to do nothing wrong is to do nothing. In this we find the elegant simplicity of all truly great ideas.

It is true that there are certain physical symbols peculiar to the high-level worker which, at a glance, would seem to run counter to the overall purpose, including such things as the car phone and the electronic beeper. A closer look, however, shows that this is not the case. There is no record of anyone using a car phone for any purpose other than to call someone who may not know you *have* a car phone and setting him straight. The beeper is even less consequential, being worn only on social occasions in singles bars, where it is considered less vulgar than affixing your income tax return to your forehead.

Talking about work while out of your element.

Despite the fact that the foregoing examples rarely vary, the amateur researcher should not assume that talking about work will be the same everywhere.

To illustrate this common pitfall, we have conducted a simple field experiment, approaching three seemingly identical places-for-the-performance-of-work in three widely separated geographic locations. Our request for a simple and common act of work was, of course, expressed in exactly the same way at each field site, with the single exception of localized greetings. Little or no knowledge of conversational Human is required to note the differences in response.

Site A.
Feldman's Music
New York, N.Y.

"Hello. I'm playing a concert tonight, and I'd like my viola bow re-haired."

"One bow you're bringing me? For this kind of business every day I'm opening at seven for what in three months is eighteen years?"

Site B.
Guitar Shack
Venice, California

"What's happenin'? I'm playing a concert tonight, and I'd like my viola bow re-haired."

"Oh, wow, yeah. The guy who does that isn't here. His old lady's like having a baby, right? So he hasn't been in for a couple of weeks 'cause he's like being with her, you know? But I think Marianne said he might be in like, I don't know, tomorrow. Hey, Marianne? MARIANNE? She must have the headphones on again. Can you check back like Thursday?"

"What's happenin'? I'm playing a concert tonight—"

"Oh, wow, yeah. You, like, said that already, right?"

Site C.
Pickers' Heaven
Buford, Alabama

"Hey how yew? I'm playing a concert tonight, and I'd like my viola bow re-haired."

"You whut?"

"What's happenin'? I'm playing—"

"You bein funny with me, boy?"

The influence on language.

At least as interesting as the ways in which work is affected by talk is the degree to which *talk*—that is, the human language itself—has been influenced by *work*. To demonstrate this, we devised one of our favorite experiments of this entire research project. Listen to this: we arranged appointments for personal interviews with two different humans, to be held at the same time and place. We chose subjects in similar, but not identical, lines of work, the better to collect a variety of work-influenced dialogue and yet ensure that they would have something to talk to each other about. (It is well-known that humans in very dissimilar lines of work will not speak except in life-threatening circumstances.) Our subjects were a food critic and a film critic, respectively. We don't really know what useful purpose either job may serve, if any, but that is, after all, irrelevant to this experiment.

The subjects were not acquainted, and neither expected the other to be there. We had rented a small apartment and furnished it in typical human style in order to put them at their ease. Then—now get this—we *never showed up* for the appointment, merely observing and recording their reactions from our hiding place in the next room. Their conversation grew more and more animated as they waited futilely for something to happen, and we gathered a wealth of material—in fact, more than we really needed, and some of it not entirely suitable for publication here. They never did figure it out, and finally just left. God, we love this stuff.

Food Critic: My first impression is of general tackiness, though the striped steel awnings and low lighting lend a certain unpretentious charm.

Film Critic: The lighting's *so* low that I wonder how we're expected to follow the action. If there's ever going to *be* any action.

FC: A nicely balanced, if slightly over furnished living room is unfortunately ruined by the bathroom, smothered in an aggressive collection of ceramic fish ornaments. The shower curtain is simply unacceptable.

FC: At least there's something in there to *look* at. I'm sorry, but this just isn't giving me enough reason to sit still for two hours.

FC: Well, I don't know. The generous couch—not overwhelmed by throw pillows, for a change—and some refreshingly naive TV trays provide a certain homey counterpoint to the cloyingly trendy color scheme.

FC: I'm glad *you* see a scheme. I'm wondering what the point is. I mean, why am I supposed to care how this turns out?

FC: Well, I admit the entry hall—really not elaborate enough to be called a foyer—would benefit from a good scrubbing.

FC: If you ask me, the whole project should have been scrubbed. This concept might have had a chance in the hands of a Griffith, a Bergman, a Signorelli. But as it is, I'm sorry.

FC: Overall, I find the experience unnecessary, yet interminable.

FC: I mean, what are they trying to say? If this is supposed to be deep and thought-provoking, it only succeeds in being murky and irritating. I'm sorry, I vote this one the stinkeroo award.

FC: I think that's the carpet freshener.

FC: No, no, you misunderstand me—

FC: On the contrary, I find you unprepossessing, yet fat and lonely.

FC: Hey, I'm sorry. This is where I came in.

FC: Maybe you'd like to take in a film?

    FC: A what?

      FC: A movie.

        FC: Oh. Sure, why not? But I could use a cheeseburger first.

        FC: A what?

          FC: Never mind. Where are you parked? Here, have a Milk Dud.

SCIENCE IN ACTION
Quiz Page

Talking about work while enjoying a quiet cocktail in a fern bar often has hidden meanings. In the situation below, does it seem most likely that

A. the male has convinced the female that she can't afford *not* to consider an add-on patio room, and she should call him Monday;

B. the female, sensing the start of something big, has asked the male for his shirt size and fragrance preferences;

C. the male is inadvertently about to show her his Piggly-Wiggly receipt for two quarts of Kaopectate.

Section Eight

Answers
and Questions

Easy answers.

Page 10.
A man and his wife.
No, and they would be silly to want it. A three-legged horse doesn't make much of a circus, but it's better that an ordinary four-legged horse. If they had planned to start a farm, as is more usual in puzzles of this sort, it would be a different story.

The old mansion.
The answer is B. It's *always* B. These people deserve what they get.

Two scalded dogs.
The truck. Or, if not, then the train.

A potato crop.
He can't. However, Old Farmer Gunderson has no intention of trying. He plans to burn the entire crop, broken-down wagon and all, and trade the horse for a Buick in which he will drive to town and cash his check from the government. He then plans to raise some serious hell.

Farmer Brown.
A farmer hat.

Surprising facts.
You're right. It was a trick question.

Optical illusions.
Policeman A is closer. B is a milkman.

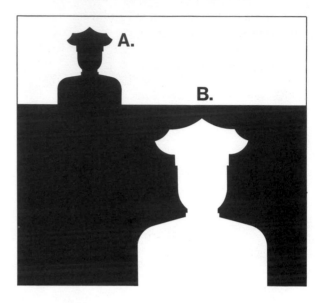

Page 20.
The only *incorrect* answer is B. What he is actually wondering is when the old baseball tradition of signing your house over to your attorney started, and why his attorney knew about it but he didn't.

Page 32.
None of the above. She is using the sports pages as an aid to decide between her final name choices: Kevin, Jason, Too-Tall, or Jésus.

Page 44.
This is very interesting. We said to put yourself in the situation, but we didn't say you had to be the patient. Do you always assume the role of the victim? A close look at your self-image is indicated. Still, as long as you did it, the correct answer is B.

Page 82.

All three theories are equally well illustrated except for B., which would have implied a Nautilus membership and designer sweats. On the other hand, it's pretty hard to tell from an artist's conception what anybody might be *considering,* so, what the hell, we'll give you B. It's not like we have to cough up a prize or anything.

Page 92.

DaBinkey also wrote, "The multiple choice question is the most pleasing to the scholar, as the longest sentence is always surely the true choice, rendering the vexation of cramming needless." History shows us that DaBinkey was a dipstick, but he knew how to psych a test.

Page 104.

Assuming you're the same person who answered on page 44, we already know that you said C. However, the question said, "does it *seem most likely* that," rendering the whole thing a matter of opinion. In other words, there *is* no answer, which is probably what you've suspected all along. So why do you keep buying those books?

Scoring curve.

If your score is up here somewhere, you did pretty well.

This can't be your score. You must not have finished.

Not so good. Looks like you'll be reading this book again next semester.

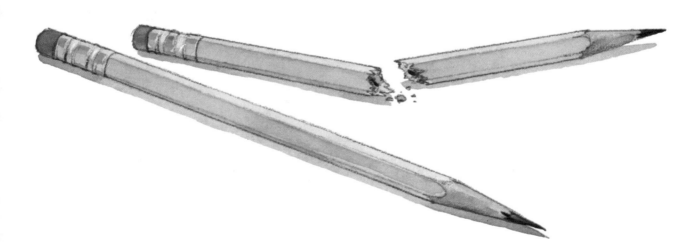

Tough questions.

Throughout our study, we have seen work as a positive force, giving shape and focus to the otherwise empty and pathetic lives of many humans. And so it is, as long as it is engaged in responsibly and in moderation. But work can be overdone and abused, all too often with tragic results. How many times, for instance, have you heard the sad disclaimer, "I can stop any time I want," as you lock your desk and straighten your cubicle, knowing that you for one have had enough, and head down to Grogan's to get plowed before catching the 7:02? How many friends have seemed to become progressively less witty and scintillating at cocktail parties and barbecues, gradually arriving later and leaving earlier, until it can no longer be ignored and they are simply not invited back? Oh, they have excuses: they've "outgrown this infantile grab-ass crowd," or they "have better things to do than discuss *Dallas* and Keogh accounts with a bunch of post-adolescent suburban wetbrains," or even, "If you want to know the truth, Bob, I just couldn't face your wife again once what we'd had between us was over." All believable enough, at first. But the time comes when they must be seen for the desperate cover-ups that they are.

It is *not* true, as has been suggested, that these people are simply weak or lacking in moral fibre. Problem working is not a character flaw. It is a disease, no different from, say, pancreatitis or cirrhosis of the liver. The answer is not recrimination or chastisement, but *understanding*. For only through understanding can we effect prevention.

The following brief questionnaire is designed to help you determine whether you may exhibit any of the early warning signs of problem working. Obviously, if your answers are less than totally honest we will all be wasting our time. Therefore, we suggest that you complete the questionnaire in privacy, and in surroundings conducive to relaxation and free from distraction. When you get there, find a place at the end and order yourself a double, straight up and hold the vegetables. Take a moment to study the tentative trickle of the condensation on the ice-cold glass, telling you that God's in his heaven and you are captain of your soul, up to maybe your third one. Then let's get this test out of the way and turn our attention to the bimbo supply.

Lately it seems to take more and more work for me to get that "high" that comes from a feeling of accomplishment.

☐ Yes. ☐ No. ☐ Okay, yes.

I like to do a little work in the morning as a "pick-me-up," especially if I've worked late the night before.

☐ Never. ☐ Sometimes. ☐ Have anything you want done? I could update these files, make a few notes. It's no bother.

I have missed cocktail parties as a result of work.

Not true. I had ☐ an out-of-town funeral ☐ a 24-hour bug of some kind ☐ car trouble.

On mornings after working late, I often can't remember:

☐ whether I turned off the copier.
☐ could you repeat the question?

I have hidden work here and there for "emergencies."

☐ Where?

I have associated with people I consider my inferiors just because they will work with me.

☐ Hold on a minute. *Where?*

When out hoisting a few with the boys, I am looking forward to getting to work.

☐ You'd understand if you knew the boys.
☐ Yo! Six more Buds here, Mama.

I become irritable if my wife suggests I'm working too much.

☐ No. ☐ Not me.
☐ *Me* irritable? That's a laugh. Why don't you get off my back, you miserable b ☐ No.

My work is approximately as important to me as:

☐ my motorcycle. ☐ my life. ☐ my genitals.

If you answered "yes" to more of these questions than offer "yes" as a choice, you may already have the beginnings of a problem. Next time work beckons, why not try staying right where you are and having just one more? You may find, as so many have, that there is always time for one more. Remember that it *is* possible to break the hold that work has on you. You just have to take one more at a time.

Why they do it: Part II

No doubt the best-known occurrence of behavior similar to human work is in the history of the Papaduron, a minor branch of the once-numerous tribes of natives inhabiting the great fibre forests of Upper Volta. The Papaduron are in no way notable for themselves, being just one more group of mud-smeared savages whose cultural zenith is the adornment of their private parts with feathers, beads, and what have you. They are of interest solely because the *specific origin* of their ritual behavior is known to modern science, due to their warriors' surprising practice of keeping detailed diaries. Thus the Papaduron are a unique textbook model for the study of atavistic ritual–behavior which continues though the original reason for it has disappeared.

The story begins near the end of the last ice age. Like other fibre forests tribes, the Papaduron were hunters. *Unlike* the other tribes, however, the men of the Papaduron were required to take the children with them on the hunt, due to the extraordinary willfulness of their women, who, for this and other reasons, are something of a legend in themselves. This presented the problem of finding some way to keep the young ones quiet while at the same time leaving the hunters' hands free for shooting game. Their solution was to require each warrior to carry two children, by clamping one head in each armpit. Though effective, this method had the drawback of limiting the mobility of the hunters' arms to below the elbow, and so led, in turn, to the next significant event.

It is at just this point in the tribe's history that we see the introduction of the diminutive bow and arrow, quite effective for shooting while the elbows are held tightly to the sides, but hardly impressive in appearance. These little bows, along with the diaries kept on a leather thong around the neck, soon became the trademark of the Papaduron warrior, and for many generations thereafter, the tiny bows, the diaries, and the fact that they had to take the kids hunting in the first place, combined to make the Papaduron the jokes of the fibre forest. To this day in the language of the neighboring tribes, the very word "Papaduron" is a derisive remark, translating roughly to, "Your weapon is maybe this big, no doubt." (accompanied by gesture with thumb and forefinger not quite touching.)

Then, as is so often the case, a chance occurrence altered the course of history. The Papaduron always brought their catch home alive, allowing the women to finish them off. (This was partly because of their non-lethal bows and arrows, and partly because the women plainly enjoyed it.) One day, one of the warriors, probably from simple force of habit, carried the game–in this case, a brace of red-footed forest chickens–in the same manner he had earlier carried the children. On arrival at the village, it was discovered that this had had the effect of irritating the normally phlegmatic birds to the point of ferocity. The unprecedented behavior of the enraged chickens enormously impressed the women, who knew nothing of life outside the village and believed the men had caught something dangerous. The Papaduron warriors had never experienced this attitude from their women, who had in fact been among the first to hold them up to general ridicule. Needless to say, this method of carrying game caught on in a big way.

We now come to the present. The Papaduron are no longer hunters, preferring to make their living by the far less strenuous method of stealing the lunches of the work crews who are engaged in the wholesale destruction of the fibre forests, from which is derived the raw material to feed the world's ever-growing demand for velcro.Thus the Papaduron find themselves in the paradoxical circumstance of having attained their greatest prosperity through a situation which is leading to their certain extinction.

Not surprisingly, however, the irony is lost on the Papaduron. They still smear themselves with mud, decorate their genitalia, and embark upon their daily raids, exactly as their ancestors did. And they return – as their ancestors did – with their spoils *tucked firmly in their armpits.* There can be no question that this is a genuine example of atavistic ritual behavior. Not only did the original motivation disappear generations ago, but the effect it was designed to produce is, of course, impossible with other than live prey. The Papaduron are primitive, but they are not so silly as to believe that any amount of rough handling will make a cheese sandwich seem more danger-ous than it is. Thus is the Papaduron's place in anthropological history assured.

Still, all of this would still have been lost to modern knowledge, had it not been for the dedication of Dr. Borkina Fasso, who lived among the declining Papaduron for seven years in an attempt to complete her doctorate. Having spent most of this time trying to teach them to shake hands, Dr. Fasso was understandably excited when one day she seemed to be on the verge of success. A tribal elder tentatively stretched his hand toward her – the result, she felt sure, of a technique she had developed of standing progressively farther away from her subject and shouting, "Put 'er there!" – when a tea strainer which she had been missing for some weeks dropped from his armpit. Before she could

react, the elder, in his embarrassment, produced what Dr. Fasso described as a "quite respectable left hook," at which her waterproof Swiss Army hand compass fell to the ground on his other side. Repairing in some haste to her hut, Dr. Fasso emerged some hours later with her now-famous conclusion: *the behavior which had begun as a necessity for their beleaguered ancestors has become so engrained that no modern male Papaduron considered himself presentable in female company without some object clutched in each armpit.* She added that, in her defense, this went a long way toward explaining the difficulty in getting them to shake hands.

We hope this enriches your understanding of the human behavior we have sought to illuminate in *Humans at Work.* If so, we feel it may be said that the passing of the Papaduron – and, for that matter, the revoking of Dr. Fasso's degree – will not have been in vain.